# CREATION, EVOLUTION AND SCIENCE

ISBN 0 9517992 1 5

Giles Printing, Langley, Norfolk
Cover design by Gabrielle Turnecliff

# CREATION EVOLUTION & SCIENCE

John V. Collyer

THE TESTIMONY
NORWICH
1993

# CONTENTS

Preface ............................................................................. 7
Acknowledgements ........................................................ 9
Introduction .................................................................. 11

## IS CREATION CREDIBLE?

1. Is the creation concept a myth? ............................. 17
2. How did life begin—by chance or design? ........... 23
3. The origin of life ....................................................... 29
4. Evidence of design in the universe ........................ 35
5. Evidence of design in Planet Earth ........................ 42
6. Evidence of design in the living cell ...................... 48
7. Evidence of design in the human brain, eyes and ears ..... 55
8. Evidence of design in bees, ants and spiders ....... 61
9. The good news at creation ...................................... 68

## IS EVOLUTION A SCIENCE?

1. Science and evolution ............................................. 79
2. Evolution and fossils ............................................... 86
3. Do mutations and natural selection produce evolution? . 92
4. Unsolved problems of evolution ............................ 98
5. The time factor ........................................................ 108
6. Theistic evolution ................................................... 119
20 scientific facts seldom taught to students ........ 127

Subject Index ............................................................... 132
Scripture Index ........................................................... 138

# PREFACE

For many years the debate between the concepts of creation and evolution was seen by the writer as much too difficult to understand for one who did not have a scientific training. While accepting the Genesis account of creation as a Divinely inspired record, the flaws in the Darwinian theory had not yet become apparent. The idea that man had descended from monkeys was regarded as a joke, with the passing thought: "Could it have been the other way round?" At this early stage in my life, the wonderful colours, designs, skills and abilities of various forms of life were appreciated, but the obvious implications were not yet realised. My elders advised me that the creation/evolution debate was so deeply scientific that it was out of my reach. "Leave it alone", they said.

Then suddenly the basic principles at stake in this debate were seen to be comparatively simple. The evidence of design, the intricate information within all forms of life, could not be the products of chance. The life style of such creatures as ants and bees was so complex that their instincts must have been produced by an intelligence. Eventually, reading Darwin's *Origin of Species* for the first time, the case for evolution was seen to be so speculative, so inconclusive, that it lost all semblance of real science. Then it was discovered that there are many other theories besides Darwin's, often pointing out his errors yet only offering further speculation. Finally, a dear young friend made biology her career. This resulted eventually in her losing faith in God's Word, in His promises and in His offer of salvation through Jesus Christ. This tragedy acted as a spur to action. Something had to be done.

Regular studies of science magazines revealed that there are numerous flaws in each of the many theories of evolution. In spite of the reported discoveries of the wonders hidden within every living cell, of the faithfulness of the genetic code, of the uniqueness of Planet Earth, it was being assumed that these were all accidents of nature, mere chance happenings. This did not make sense to me, and I soon found that it did not make sense to many others too.

The many theories of evolution, with new ones cropping up almost every year, each in turn finding fault with earlier theories, showed that the concept of evolution had become self-defeating. On the other hand, the record of creation in Genesis was found to be wholly consistent with observed science, upheld throughout the Bible, and the basis for the Creator's purpose for the earth and its life. This work is an attempt to share this view of the scene, as seen by a non-scientist, with others who may have been bamboozled by the scientific jargon used by evolutionists.

*John V. Collyer*

# ACKNOWLEDGEMENTS

The material for this book was first published as a series of articles by Brother John Collyer in *The Testimony* magazine during 1990 and 1991. It was decided by the Testimony Committee to issue them in book form. The text has been revised, and several diagrams and other material added.

Thanks are due to Brethren John Watts and Tony Benson, and to Mr John Adds, Senior Lecturer in Biology at Chelmsford College of Further Education, for their helpful criticisms and corrections. However, the final responsibility for the text lies with Brother Collyer and myself.

We are also grateful to Sister Mary Benson, who prepared the text for printing, Brethren David and Jim Willey, who produced the line drawings and diagrams, Sister Gill Nicholls, who compiled the index, and Sister Gabrielle Turnecliff, who designed the cover.

*John Nicholls*

# INTRODUCTION

Here we are, on Planet Earth, with innumerable forms of life all around us. The essentials for life to be continued by reproduction, and for each new generation to be sustained, are normally available. It is so easy to take for granted the basic needs of all forms of life: the air, the sunlight, the water and the nutrients which have been provided. Life on earth is only possible because of a whole series of favourable coincidences. The natural question for a thoughtful mind is, How has this extraordinary state of affairs come about?

This question has produced three alternative answers, all of which have their advocates; yet only one of the answers can be the correct one.

1. That the planet was prepared for the reception of life before any life was placed upon it by the Creator. That life was created by the Creator, the Living God, in a specific logical order of creation. That the purpose of creation was revealed to man in the simple and straightforward account of creation that has been written down and preserved down the ages in the Bible. That creation cannot be repeated by human contrivance, or scientific experiment, hence cannot be scientifically proved by re-enaction. Hence, belief in creation is a matter of faith in the Creator's record.

2. That this planet happened to be a suitable site for the natural elements to somehow become organised into a simple form of life. In the course of millions of years this simple life evolved into the vast complexity of life that is evident today. This is called the theory of evolution, of which there are many variations, none of which has been proved scientifically, as the process cannot be repeated. Hence, belief in evolution is a matter of faith in an inexplicable process which is still hotly debated.

3. That this planet was prepared by a supernatural agency (God) for the reception of life. That a simple primitive form of life was implanted on earth, having the inherent capacity to develop into the many forms of life to be found on the planet today. This is known as theistic evolution, and is intended to unite the concept of a supernatural creation with the theory of evolution, bringing together the Bible and science.

That life should suddenly spring from non-life, a process called 'spontaneous generation', as is assumed for most theories of evolution, would be a miracle. That it is not a natural process, and has not been repeated, was proved by the experiments of that eminent scientist, Louis Pasteur, over a century ago.

That life should be an act of creation by a superhuman Creator, as recorded in the Bible (and as retold in many ancient myths), would also be a miracle. Creation cannot be explained as a naturally occurring process, even though re-creation is taking place in a million ways all over the planet all the time. That life only comes from life is known as the Law of Biogenesis. Curiously the very name of this basic law of nature was coined by a well-known evolutionist: "The hypothesis that living matter always arises by the agency of pre-existing living matter... I shall call Biogenesis".[1]

Thus neither the evolution of life from non-life, nor the creation of life by a living Creator, can be explained as a natural process. To believe either proposition is an act of faith:
1. faith in a process that has been shown to be unscientific at its base (for the origin of life is not known to science); or
2. faith in the Creator, Who has explained His creation and its purpose in His treatise, the Bible.

As neither process can be proved scientifically by repetition, to opt for either concept requires faith.

For any concept to be credible there have to be good reasons for believing it. In the first part of this book we look at some good reasons for believing that special creation is a reasonable scientific concept. It is hoped to demonstrate that science and the Bible are in agreement. In the second part we look at the scientific reasons that are offered in support of the theory of evolution in the light of pronouncements of eminent evolutionists, and then at the theory of theistic evolution in the light of the Bible and science.

*"I THINK that we must go further than this and admit the only acceptable explanation—creation. I know that this is anathema to physicists, as indeed it is to me, but we must not reject a theory that we do not like if the experimental evidence supports it"* ("A Physicist Looks at Evolution", Lipson, *Physics Bulletin 31*, 1980, p. 138).

•

**A REVIEW** of a book by Sir Nevil Mott states: *"In the U.S.A. over a fourth of scientists are active in churches, and half describe themselves as religious. Science and theology represent two complementary ways of looking at reality. The essential message of this volume is that science is not legitimately an obstacle to religious belief"* (*Nature*, 11 April 1991, p. 528). The history of science reveals that many of the pioneer scientists believed the Bible, with its definitive account of Divine creation.

•

**JAMES CLERK MAXWELL,** the Scottish physicist who propounded the electromagnetic theory of light, in a lecture at Aberdeen, told his students *"to know, to submit to, and to fulfil the laws which the Author of the Universe has appointed"*. Maxwell was one of many pioneer scientists who sought to honour the Creator (*Nature*, 17 January 1991, p. 201).

•

*"THE origin of the Solar System from a rotating disk of gas and dust is becoming well understood—or so it is generally believed . . . we are no longer sure that we know how the Solar System formed, but are just beginning to realise how much there is which we still need to learn"*, says Joe Nath of NASA (*Nature*, 3 January 1991, p. 18). It is good to see this acknowledgement of official ignorance on a subject that the public thinks has been scientifically established.

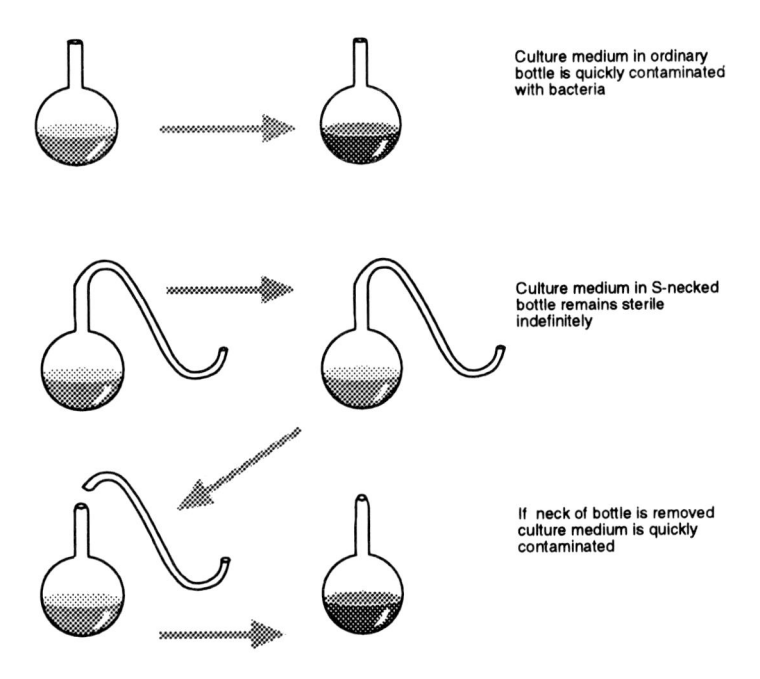

Pasteur's experiments disproving the spontaneous generation of microorganisms. Sugar and yeast were placed in flasks and boiled to kill bacteria. Flasks with straight necks allowed bacteria to settle into the culture, and it was quickly teeming with bacteria. The S-shaped neck did not permit bacteria to enter, and, though the flask was open to the air, its contents did not become contaminated unless the neck was removed.

Most of the quotations will be from the works of scientists who are evolutionists. However, it is far from true that all scientists are in favour of the theory of evolution, and there are some eminent men of all branches of science do not support the theory. While a few of these will be quoted, the writer wishes to avoid giving the impression that the quotations are unduly biased.

### References
1. T. H. Huxley (1870), *Lay Sermons*, p. 350.

# IS CREATION CREDIBLE?

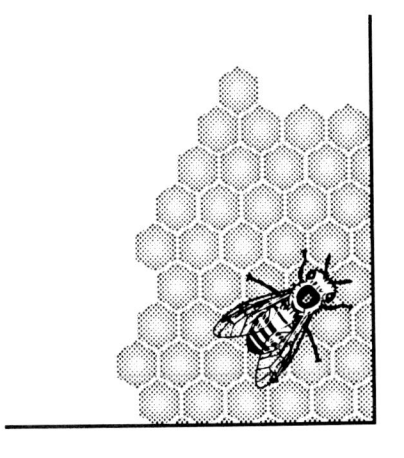

# 1

## IS THE CREATION CONCEPT A MYTH?

It has been frequently alleged by critics of the Bible that the account of creation in Genesis is a Hebrew myth, borrowed from the Babylonian mythology at the time when the Jews were exiles in that land. For example, Lewis Spence wrote: "The Hebrew account of the successive stages of creation corresponds so closely to that of Babylon, that it is obvious one has been influenced by the other".[1] He then continues with the comment: "... naturally the younger by the older". However, he does not say which he thinks was the younger, or which the older, leaving it to the reader to make whichever assumption he prefers. The atheist will assume that the Hebrew account was borrowed from the Babylonians; but it would be equally reasonable to take the alternative view.

What is a myth? As with so many English words that describe abstract ideas, it comes from a Greek word, *mythos*. This means a legend, folklore or a traditional narrative that has an element of fact hidden in an adornment of fiction. Myths should not be dismissed as baseless stories. Within many of them is hidden an historical fact or event, which has been termed the 'mythoplasm'. This germ of fact may be so overlaid with elaboration that the mythoplasm can be quite difficult to discern.

### What is hiding in the myths?
Several extensive studies of the myths of ancient people have been undertaken. Perhaps the best known and most extensive is *The Golden Bough* by Sir James G. Frazer. More recent studies include

*Folklore as an Historical Science* by Sir G. L. Gomme, and *Introduction to Mythology*, cited above. It is not proposed to get involved in mythology, but only to make references that clear Genesis of the accusation that it is a myth. Gomme points out that "In front of the legends attaching to persons and places is the history of these persons and places".[2] To put this assessment in other words, there is a basis of fact hiding behind the embroidery of a typical myth or legend. The problem is to find that basis of fact—the mythoplasm.

A careful reading of the first chapter of Genesis will fail to find any trace of the typical myth. It is a factual account, without any embroidery. As Kenneth Kitchen of Liverpool University wrote: "The common assumption that the Hebrew account is simply a purged and simplified version of the Babylonian legend is wrong on methodological grounds. The rule is that the simple accounts or traditions may give rise to elaborate legends, but not vice versa. In the ancient Orient, legends were not simplified ... as assumed for early Genesis".[3] C. F. von Weizsacker compares the Hebrew account of the origin of the earth and the life upon it with the various myths of Babylon, Greece and Iceland. He shows clearly that Genesis is anti-mythical, and is a factual record, quite unlike a typical myth.[4] These highly imaginative creation myths of the ancients may well have a foundation of fact, the mythoplasm. Researchers have traced hundreds of creation myths from every continent. Many of them have certain features in common. More importantly, none of them depict man as having evolved from an animal.

The Babylonian creation myth has been epitomised thus: "Marduk used the two halves of Tiamat to create the firmament of heaven and earth. He then set in order the stars, sun and moon. Lastly, to free the gods from menial tasks, Marduk, with the help of Ea, created mankind from the clay mingled with the blood of Kingu, the rebel god who had led Tiamat's forces".[5]

The Sumerian myth, known as the *Enuma Elish* (meaning 'When from above') is also of interest. The relevant part of it has been rendered like this:

"Let Nintu mix clay,
So let god and man be mingled together in the clay.
After she had mixed the clay,

# IS THE CREATION CONCEPT A MYTH? 19

She called Anuna, the great gods.
Then Igugu the great god spat upon the clay.
Mami opened her mouth and said to the great gods,
You commanded me a task and I have finished it,
I have removed your toil,
I have imposed your load upon man".

### Where is the mythoplasm?

As with all the creation myths, 'the gods' were involved. The event is seen as superhuman; man is created by a supernatural agency. In the above examples, as in many other myths, man is formed of clay, or earth. A comparison with the simple words of Genesis 2:7 should be enough to emphasise both the similarity and the difference in the two accounts: "the LORD God formed man of the dust of the ground, and breathed into his nostrils the breath of life; and man became a living soul".

The similarity is most noticeable in that both Genesis and myth speak of a supernatural event, and of the earthy composition of man. The difference between the simple statement of Genesis and the elaborate and imaginative description in the myth is very marked. Thus the hidden mythoplasm of the myth is in fact a confirmation of the underlying facts of the creation account in Genesis. It is highly unlikely that ancient people all over the world would have similar myths of creation unless this event was the mythoplasm common to all of them. That such similar concepts should have arisen spontaneously worldwide is highly improbable. The simple record of Genesis provides the facts of history upon which the worldwide myths of creation have developed in all their many variations.

Another glance at the worldwide creation myths will reveal yet another mythoplasm. Nearly all of them begin by describing the earth as a vast world of waters over which the creative agency brooded. Then by a spoken word, or by force of thought, the dry land was raised from the midst of the watery abyss. For example, the Egyptian god of creation, known as Khepera, created the world "out of his mouth", that is, by his spoken word. The Peruvian deity, Pacacamac, made all things "by his word". These, and other similar

*"**APART** from being philosophically unacceptable, the Big Bang is an over-simple view of how the Universe began, and it is unlikely to survive the decade ahead. In all respects, save that of convenience, this view of the origin of the Universe is thoroughly unsatisfactory . . . It is an effect whose cause cannot be identified, or even discussed"* (Nature, 10 August 1989, p. 425). It is a bold science writer who denounces the currently popular theory of the origin of the universe. How soon will students be told that this theory is now outdated?

•

*"**IF GOD** was smart enough to create the system he was certainly smart enough to cover his tracks, that is he could have 'implanted' the geological astronomical record so that what many of us now see as a scientifically pre-Creation history, is merely a divine artefact. I say this as a non-creationist scientist, who nevertheless cannot find a way around this argument. We simply believe that there was no relatively recent Creation, but cannot prove it. Can you? If not, then science would appear to be a religion"* (Nature, 15 December 1988, p. 614). This candid admission by a scientist raises an interesting point. Adam and Eve were created as mature beings, not babies. Plants, trees and animals were all created mature and seed-bearing. Why should not the planet also have been made mature and ready for life? As the writer suggests, evolution is a 'faith' in something unproven.

•

*"**THE BIG** Bang theory suggests that the red shift of an object depends on its distance from us . . . maybe the red shift has nothing to do with distance"* (New Scientist, 2 March 1991, p. 48). This article is of interest in that it discounts current theories, and offers alternatives, but none offer Divine creation as the logical origin of the universe.

# IS THE CREATION CONCEPT A MYTH? 21

variations of the creation myths, appear to be faint echoes of the Biblical "And God said", words which occur in Genesis 1. Creation is summarised in the words of Psalm 33:6: "By the word of the LORD were the heavens made; and all the host of them by the breath of His mouth". It is amazing to find the myths confirming the details of the Genesis account in this way, the legends agreeing with the true history.

### Is it all imaginary?

It can be asked, As no man had yet been created, how could the early works of the creation be accurately described? This is a good question, which needs a good answer. The myths fail to give the answer; the Bible does provide it. It points out that there were actually witnesses of the events, albeit superhuman witnesses. In Job 38 God enumerates some of the wonders of His creation in order to humble the man Job. Then in verse 7 God says that "all the sons of God shouted for joy" at creation. As man had not yet been made, who were these "sons of God"? The answer is that they were the Divine angels who "excel in strength, that do His commandments, hearkening unto the voice of His word" (Ps. 103:20). The word translated "God" in Genesis 1 is the Hebrew word *elohim*, meaning 'mighty ones'. The same Hebrew word is translated "gods" again in Psalm 97:7, and this is quoted in Hebrews 1:6 as "angels".

Thus we learn that the creative work was carried out by the Divine angels in accordance with the Divine Creator's word, or instruction. The Creator was the architect with the power and the knowledge, while the angels were His craftsmen. Thus it was fitting that the angels should take delight in the wonderful work of creation in which they had taken part. In due course it was by the angels that God spoke to men; hence the record of Genesis is a true record transmitted by angels to men. Genesis is by no means just a myth.

As the creation record in Genesis was accepted as a true record by the Divinely inspired writers of the Bible, and endorsed by none other than Jesus Christ, it must not be dismissed as a primitive Hebrew myth. Indeed, the whole of the Divine purpose for the earth and for man, as revealed in the Bible, is based upon the events of the Genesis record. Disbelief in Genesis results in a future of hopelessness for both the planet and its passengers.

**References**

1. Lewis Spence (1921), *Introduction to Mythology*, Harrap, London, p. 167.
2. Sir G. L. Gomme (1904), *Folklore as an Historical Science*, Antiquarian Books, p. 148.
3. K. Kitchen (1966), *Ancient Orient and the Old Testament*, Tyndale Press, p. 89.
4. C. F. von Weizsacker (1964), *The Relevance of Science*, London.
5. *The New Bible Dictionary* (1962), IVF Press, p. 273.

# 2

# HOW DID LIFE BEGIN—BY CHANCE OR DESIGN?

A noted biologist has written: "The evidence of those who would explain life's origin on the basis of the accidental combination of suitable chemical elements, is no more tangible than that of those people who place their faith in divine creation as the explanation of the development of life. Obviously the latter have as much justification for their belief as do the former".[1]

The big question is, Could life be the product of a whole series of chance occurrences, of accidents of nature, without any plan or purpose, as envisaged by proponents of the theory of evolution? Or was life purposed, designed and created by a super-power with super-intelligence and super-abilities? These are the main alternatives to the problem of how life on earth began, with all its complexity, and with its interdependence of one form of life upon another, with its orderliness and its beauty. The choice is between chance or design.

That this is the view of a thoughtful evolutionist may be seen in the conclusion reached by the writer of a 400-page defence of the theory of evolution: "It must certainly be admitted that miraculous creation is compatible with what we know. There is no way of disproving the claim that new species were created . . . On the other hand, there is no way of proving that miracles occurred, or even that they can occur, because supernatural events of this kind do not appear to have taken place during the period of recorded human history".[2]

### Does it matter?

Does it really matter which view one takes? Since it is true that neither evolution nor creation can be proved scientifically by being re-enacted, why should one not adopt whichever view is preferred? That the two concepts are diametrically opposed is made clear by the statement of Professor T. H. Huxley that "The doctrine of evolution, if consistently accepted, makes it impossible to believe the Bible". In a booklet by Woolsey Teller of the Humanist Society, entitled *Evolution Implies Atheism*, it is clearly stated that "The God idea cannot be reconciled with our knowledge of evolution".

Thus the gauntlet has been thrown down, the challenge has been made. The choice is either the one or the other, chance or design, an accident of nature or the purpose of the Creator. That the choice is a serious one for each individual only becomes evident when it is realised how that choice affects one's way of thinking, philosophy of life and moral behaviour. A very perceptive scientist, Professor J. Holmes, wrote: "Few people who accept the Darwinian theory of evolution realise its far-reaching import, especially in social science . . . Darwinism consistently applied would measure goodness in terms of survival value . . . our ethics are Darwinian, whether we like it or not".[3]

That these observations have turned out to be true can be seen in the history of this century in the lowering of moral standards, the abandonment of faith and the survival of the fittest in the world of commerce. To the Chinese people Darwin is not the father of evolution but a moral philosopher. To them he was the great propounder of the principle that might is right.[4] It was Professor T. H. Huxley who wrote: "it was cunning and ruthlessness that enabled man to evolve from the beasts"; and: "it is the law of the jungle that has to be the directive for all so-called human progress". The ultimate consequence of this philosophy has been well expressed in the words, "Man's inhumanity to man makes countless thousands mourn". In other words, the philosophy of evolution comes to a dead end. It offers no hope for a better future.

In complete contrast, the Christian ethic taught by Jesus leads to the conclusion that "the meek . . . shall inherit the earth", and, "to

# HOW DID LIFE BEGIN?

*"THE WAY cells divide into two identical copies has been well known for nearly a century. But only now are scientists beginning to understand what orchestrates this marvellous process . . . One protein is the major regulator in virtually all organisms"* (*Scientific American*, March 1991, p. 34). 'Orchestration' is not a product of chance. The more that science reveals about the wonders of the living cell, the more obvious it becomes that it was meticulously designed by the Creator.

•

**PLANTS** recognise their molecular signature: *"When a pollen grain lands on a flower, fertilization does not always follow. The plant may accept some pollen grains, but reject others . . . this selection procedure is far from random. It relies on precise genetic mechanisms, which in turn depend on a single gene, known as the S gene"* (*New Scientist*, 16 September 1989, p. 30). Notice that the process is *"far from random"*, that is, it is not a matter of chance, but of choice. The flower was 'programmed' when it was created so that it would be true that its "seed was in itself, after his kind" (Gen. 1:12).

•

**A BACTERIUM** replies to humans: *"We are not nearly as simple as we may seem to you. We can pack more biochemical versatility into a couple of cubic micrometers than you can in a couple of kgs. of liver, kidney and other offal. We do not need hearts and lungs, as we breathe by diffusion. With propellers more efficient than yours, we can swim at speeds exceeding a thousand lengths a minute. To fly, we don't need wings . . . we just get blown about effortlessly and thereby we can get anywhere"* (*Nature*, 14 January 1991, p. 97). The deeper we can look into the secrets of microscopic life, the more amazing becomes God's wonderful world.

this man will I look, even to him that is poor and of a contrite spirit, and trembleth at My word" (Mt. 5:5; Isa. 66:2). Creation of life on a prepared earth is seen as the beginning of the great preparation when eventually, in spite of man's folly and opposition, "as truly as I live, all the earth shall be filled with the glory of the LORD" (Num. 14:21). To fulfil this Divine objective it is necessary "to make ready a people prepared for the Lord" (Lk. 1:17). The creation of life on earth is seen as being purposeful and meaningful, as the conscious and deliberate work of the everliving God, Who so loves life that He wishes to share His kind of life with all those characters who emulate His Son, Jesus, on this glorified and purified planet, in the near future, when Jesus returns to take control.

### A logical sequence

The evolutionist sees the development of life as a sequence from the first living cell through increasingly complex forms of life up to man. However, evolutionists freely admit that the origin of the first living cell is not known to science, nor is the mechanism by which the process of evolution may have taken place. Numerous theories have been proposed, but there is no agreement by science as to how or when evolution took place. Nevertheless, it is claimed as a fact.

The account of creation in Genesis is a very concise statement of an essentially logical sequence of how increasingly complex forms of life were created, and placed on a planet that had been well prepared for life. The prime necessities for life—earth, water, air, light and warmth—preceded the creation of vegetation. In turn vegetation was prepared as the necessary food of living creatures. This logical sequence may be the only factor in which the two concepts can be in agreement.

The creation record differs radically from evolution in that each form of life was made complete from the beginning, and "God saw that it was good" (Gen. 1:12,21,25). There was therefore no need for change from one kind of life to another. This was ensured by the provision, "whose seed was in itself" (Gen. 1:12)—the first pronouncement of the scientific Law of Biogenesis. Some critics of the Bible try to confuse the issue by stating that there are two mutually contradictory accounts of creation in the first two chapters of

# HOW DID LIFE BEGIN?

Genesis. This is a very superficial criticism. Chapter two is not a restatement of the sequence of creation, but is an introduction to the events that follow, and the vital relationship between the Creator and the man He had made.

## Two philosophies

The alternatives of evolution or creation, of chance or design, are much more than a choice between an undervalued Bible and a glorified science. The choice is between two philosophies: the Divine philosophy of a positive purpose for life, and the atheistic and negative philosophy of the survival of the fittest, with its continued violence, ruthlessness, destruction and hopelessness. While some people claim that man will solve his problems through the advances of science, the record of history is that science is largely to blame for causing the problems that are accruing. Pollution of the planet; the extinction of species; the threat of a nuclear holocaust—these are some of the fruits of the philosophy of evolution, and the way in which it has influenced science.

It is commonly claimed that evolution is scientific, with the obvious inference that the concept of creation cannot be scientific. It may be as well to ask, What is science? A simple dictionary definition is, "Knowledge that deals with material beings, things and phenomena. Natural history in a wide sense". Hence a scientific theory is a proposed scheme that is intended to agree with observed facts, and to be a rational evaluation of them. Thus both evolution and creation could be claimed to be scientific theories, for both claim to be in agreement with the facts of nature, and both are intended to be a rational explanation of how life on earth originated and developed.

Yet it has to be admitted that neither of these theories can be proved scientifically by exact observation or by replication. In view of this fact, perhaps it would be honest to admit that neither of the theories are strictly scientific, although science can be brought to bear in considering the merits of each concept. It is not true that this subject is beyond the understanding of the average reader. Though the evolutionist may try to 'blind with science' by using unfamiliar language, it is intended to try to keep this book within the ready understanding of a non-technical person.

**References**
1. H. J. Fuller (1941), *The Plant World*, Holt & Co., New York, p. 20.
2. P. J. Bowler (1984), *Evolution—the History of an Idea*, University of California Press, p. 342.
3. *Science* (14 Aug. 1939), p. 117.
4. *New Scientist* (16 Aug. 1984), p. 35.

# 3

# THE ORIGIN OF LIFE

Life on earth is plainly stated in the Bible to have originated from the work of the Divine Creator, Who formed the earth and filled it with all manner of life, all life having the ability to replicate itself. The living God created living things; life came from life, in keeping with the scientifically observed Law of Biogenesis. That is not to say that God created *ex nihilo*, out of nothing, for "the Spirit of God moved" (Gen. 1:2) to perform this great work, and the all-powerful Spirit of God should not be described as "nothing".

The origin of life on earth is not known to the evolutionist. This fact was freely admitted to the assembled scientists of the Royal Society at their annual meeting at Liverpool in November 1981 by their president Sir Andrew Huxley. After expounding on the theory of evolution, he drew attention to the gaps in the theory, which he said included the problem of the origin of life, and the existence of consciousness, "too often swept under the carpet".[1]

For many centuries, due to faulty observation, it was thought that life was generated spontaneously. Dead flesh was seen to breed maggots. The previous attentions of the blowfly had not been noted. Also, life was thought to emerge spontaneously from mud, because the life cycle of the many small creatures in the mud was unknown. Even though Louis Pasteur and others showed, by sterilising food in a sealed container, that life could not spring from non-life, yet the idea of spontaneous generation persisted.

That the problem of the origin of life was seen as a great obstacle to the acceptance of the theory of evolution is evident from the writing of Haeckel, who wrote: "The origin of the first monera [single cell] by spontaneous generation appears to us a necessary event in the process of the development of the Earth. We admit that this process, as long as it is not directly observed or repeated by experiment, remains pure hypothesis. But I must say again that this hypothesis is indispensable for the consistent non-miraculous history of creation".[2] Would spontaneous generation be "non-miraculous"? Since Pasteur established scientifically that life cannot proceed from non-life, surely spontaneous generation would indeed be a miracle.

### Was it spontaneous generation or life from space?

Numerous attempts have been made to make the molecules of living cells in a test tube, in order to prove that life could arise spontaneously from non-life. Probably the best known of these experiments was that of Miller and Urey. These scientists tried to repeat the conditions of the 'primeval soup' in which Darwin speculated that life might have evolved. They did succeed in making a tarry substance in which four of the twenty amino acids that occur in life had been formed. This gave rise to press reports that life had been made in a test tube.

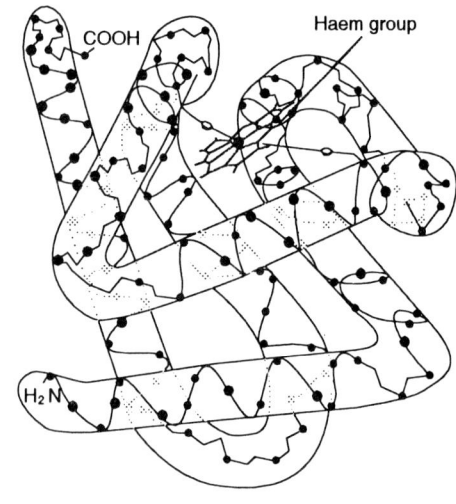

The structure of myoglobin, containing 153 amino acids.

Many other scientists have succeeded in synthesising other amino acids, but it was at the expense of much thought, contrivance and skill. Such procedures are by no means spontaneous generation, and are a long way from chance occurrence. Even if all the twenty amino acids of life were synthesised, that would not be life, for a living cell is much more than that. The fact is that a can of meat

# THE ORIGIN OF LIFE

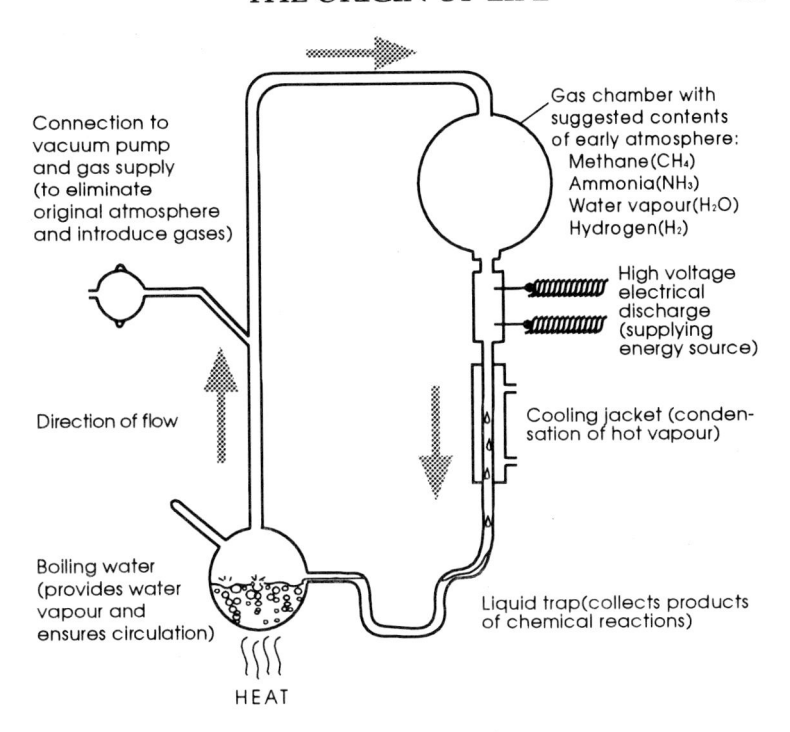

**Connection to vacuum pump and gas supply** (to eliminate original atmosphere and introduce gases)

**Gas chamber with suggested contents of early atmosphere:** Methane($CH_4$) Ammonia($NH_3$) Water vapour($H_2O$) Hydrogen($H_2$)

**High voltage electrical discharge** (supplying energy source)

**Direction of flow**

**Cooling jacket** (condensation of hot vapour)

**Boiling water** (provides water vapour and ensures circulation)

**Liquid trap** (collects products of chemical reactions)

**HEAT**

Stanley Miller's apparatus, in which he synthesised amino acids from gases under conditions thought to have been present in the primeval atmosphere. A total of fifteen amino acids was isolated.

has all the ingredients of life in it, but it is beyond the men of science to bring it to life.

In 1990 the headline "Artificial molecule shows 'sign of life'" appeared.[3] It was reported that "the first synthetic molecule that can form copies of itself has been made in the U.S. The new molecule is far simpler than biological molecules that can replicate themselves, such as DNA". To say that it showed a 'sign of life' was a gross overstatement, no doubt to lift the sagging case for evolution. This experiment, like the others, required the right molecules to be made available at the right time and in the right place, and was by no means an example of chance.

Realising the impossibility of life being produced from non-life, some evolutionists have proposed other theories. One of these has been to push the problem into outer space by suggesting that the first life arrived on earth by means of star dust, or by hitching a lift on a meteorite. When some scientists were examining a meteorite to test this theory, they were excited to find traces of amino acids. But their hopes faded when it was finally realised that the sweaty hands of the scientists had provided the traces.[4]

**What about other theories?**

Scientists who are looking for other theories are vociferous in pointing out the deficiencies of Darwinism. Indeed, some of the harshest critics of the theory of evolution are evolutionists who have a new theory of their own to offer. They are not slow to point out where Lamarck, or Darwin, or other theorists, were wrong, so that to learn the weak points of a theory one needs only to consult the writings of the latest theorists.

Evolutionists who are dissatisfied with Darwin's theory have made various suggestions, such as the chance blending of gases under unknown favourable conditions eventually forming life, or even the accidental getting together of two molecules of clay in a meaningful way. The situation was summed up by the American scientist Hubert P. Yockey: "One must conclude that, contrary to the current and established wisdom, a scenario describing the genesis of life on earth by chance and natural causes, which can be accepted on the basis of fact and not faith, has not yet been written".[5] This squarely leaves the evolutionist as a believer in something that is quite unknown, that cannot be proved and that is unrepeatable. This surely means that to accept the theory of evolution is a matter of faith. That is not science by any reckoning; it is philosophy.

---

**QUESTION:** How many polypeptides, 100 amino acids in length (a modest length for a protein), could be made using all twenty common amino acids?

**ANSWER:** $20^{100} = 1.27 \times 10^{130}$. This is much larger than the number of atoms in the universe (estimated at about $10^{100}$). Thus there is effectively an infinite potential for variation among protein structures.

## The Tree of Evolution

*A tree without roots, propped up by theories*

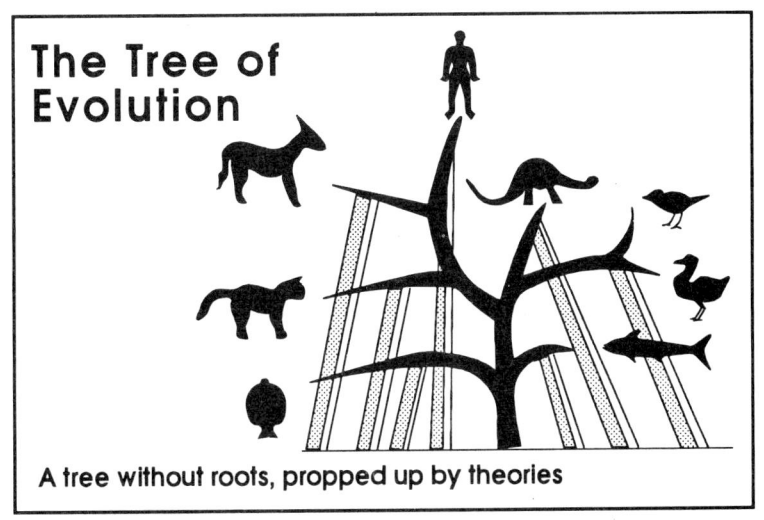

A book by Robert Shapiro, *Origins*,[6] offers a tourist guide to the various competing theories of how life originated, and very successfully debunks each one. This exercise, however, is but the preliminary to offering his own new theory. Another book on a similar theme, *The Creation of Life, Past, Future, Alien* by Andrew Scott,[7] gives a sober appraisal of the competing ideas and the scarcity of facts on which those ideas are based, but offers no alternative. In spite of their titles, both books leave the reader no wiser than when he began, except to realise that science is completely ignorant of the origin of life.

In an article in *New Scientist*, entitled "A New Paradigm for Evolution",[8] the writer pointed out that "the primary question for evolutionary theory is how life itself emerged", and then made the significant comment: "The particular conjunction of atoms that are necessary for life seem to be exceedingly improbable". It is clear that, from the point of view of science, the elaborate evolutionary 'tree' which decorates students' text-books is a tree without roots, and is only propped up by the numerous theories of evolution. By contrast, the concept of Divine creation, as so clearly stated in Genesis, is in keeping with the scientific Law of Biogenesis, that life only proceeds from life. All living forms upon earth had their origin at the behest of the Living Creator, Who "giveth to all life, and breath, and all things" (Acts 17:25).

**References**

1. *Nature* (3 Dec. 1981), p. 395.
2. Professor E. Haeckel (1892), *History of Creation*, Kegan Paul, p. 348.
3. *New Scientist* (28 Apr. 1990), p. 38.
4. *New Scientist* (5 Jan. 1986), p. 34.
5. *Journal of Theoretical Biology* (1977), No. 67, p. 396.
6. Robert Shapiro (1980), *Origins*, Heinemann, London.
7. Andrew Scott (1986), *The Creation of Life, Past, Future, Alien*, Basil Blackwell.
8. *New Scientist* (27 Feb. 1987), p. 41.

# 4

# EVIDENCE OF DESIGN IN THE UNIVERSE

Sir James Jeans, the eminent astronomer-scientist who did so much to popularise the study of the heavens, wrote: "A scientific study of the universe has suggested a conclusion which may be summed up in the statement that the universe appears to have been designed by a pure mathematician". Then he continued: "Everything points with overwhelming force to a definite creation, or series of events of creation at some time, or times not infinitely remote . . . The universe cannot have originated by chance out of the present ingredients, neither can it always have been the same as now".[1]

The world-famous scientist, Professor Albert Einstein, renowned for his Theory of Relativity, wrote: "The scientist's religious feeling takes the form of a rapturous amazement at the harmony of natural law, which reveals an intelligence of such superiority that, compared with it, all the systematic thinking and acting of human beings is an utterly insignificant reflection".[2] Dr Paul Davies of Kings College, London wrote: "Everywhere we look in the universe, from the far-flung galaxies to the deepest recesses of the atom, we encounter order . . . if information and order always have a natural tendency to disappear (in keeping with the Second Law of Thermodynamics) where did all the information that makes the world such a special place come from originally?".[3]

### Whose hand?

This is a good question, which demands an answer. The Bible answers it quite clearly, for information can only proceed from an

*"**ONLY** planets offer the platform where advanced life can develop and evolve. If ours is the only Solar System in the galaxy, then ours is also the only civilisation in the galaxy. Astronomers have yet to detect a single planet beyond the nine that orbit the sun"* (*New Scientist*, 25 May 1991, p. 59). Here is scientific evidence that our planet is unique, and life on our planet is unique, which should make the intelligent observer ask, Why?

●

*"**ALL** science is based on the assumption that the physical world is ordered. The most powerful expression of order is found in the laws of physics. Nobody knows where these laws came from, nor why they operate universally and unfailingly, but we see them at work all around us"* (*New Scientist*, 6 October 1990, p. 48). It is not true that nobody knows where these laws came from, although they are a puzzle to evolutionists. The article then raises the question as to how erratic events such as storms and earthquakes fit into a world of order, and suggests a new theory of chaos. The overruling power of God is beyond the understanding of an atheist. He sees the theory of chaos as freeing him from law and order.

●

*"**THE** standard big bang model is based on a circular argument, and difficulties with that model stem from a failure to break out of the circle"* (*New Scientist*, 3 August 1991, p. 16). The Big Bang theory, unscientific though it is, seems to have caught the popular imagination and will be difficult to erase.

●

*"**EVERYWHERE** we look in the Universe we encounter order; where did all the information that makes the world such a special place come from originally?"* (*New Scientist*, 1978, p. 506). To this vital question science has no answer, but the Bible has.

# DESIGN IN THE UNIVERSE

intelligence: "Who hath measured the waters in the hollow of his hand, and meted out heaven with the span, and comprehended the dust of the earth in a measure, and weighed the mountains in scales, and the hills in a balance? Who hath directed the Spirit of the LORD, or being His counsellor hath taught Him?" (Isa. 40:12,13). The amazing picture of the Creator measuring the oceans, which seems to suggest a remote and unknowable hidden power, follows a very touching picture of the same Creator in the previous verse: "He shall feed His flock like a shepherd: He shall gather the lambs with His arm, and carry them in His bosom, and shall gently lead those that are with young". Thus the creation concept is not of an impersonal 'First Cause', but of a Creator Who cares for His creation, as has been seen by the very extensive and complete preparations made on the planet before any life was created.

That pioneer scientist, Sir Isaac Newton, well known for his first enunciation of the Law of Gravity, wrote in *Principia*: "This most beautiful system of the sun, planets and comets, could only proceed from the counsel and dominion of an intelligent and powerful Being". This observation was based on his own discovery, which in turn was founded upon Kepler's laws on the regular movements of the planets. Johannes Kepler had written: "I feel carried away and possessed by an unutterable rapture over the divine spectacle of the heavenly harmony".

It is not without reason that astronomers have been awed at their observations and discoveries of the wonders of the universe, in which our planet is but a speck. Professor P. Dirac of Cambridge University wrote: "God is a mathematician of a very high order, and He used very advanced mathematics in constructing the Universe".[4] That is a practical scientist's way of denying that the universe is a product of chance, and confirming that it is the result of deliberate design and construction by a supernatural power. It is the mathematical precision of the universe that has enabled space scientists to make the essential calculations to send probes into space to examine the other planets of the solar system. If the universe was the product of chance occurrences, or accidents of nature, it would be in a state of chaos, whereas there is mathematical order and precision. This fact alone should be enough to make one realise that there is purpose in the universe, and to make an open mind seek for the cause of that purpose.

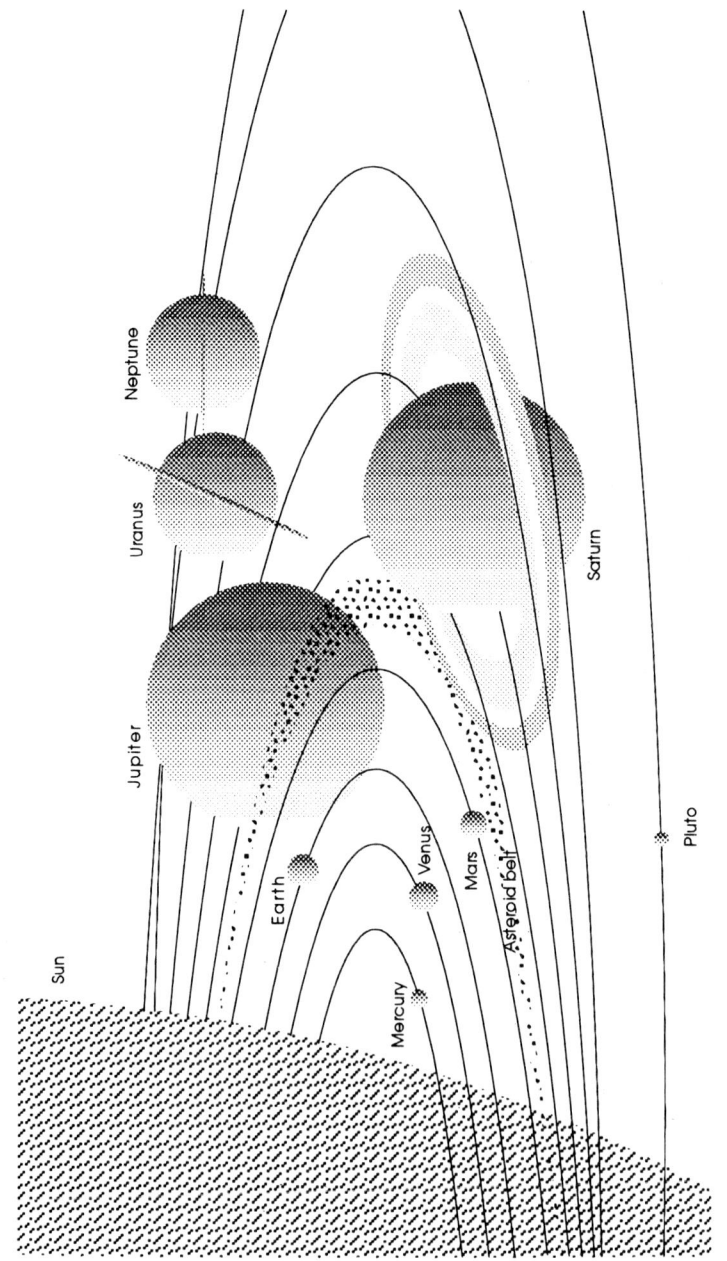

Our Solar System (distances not to scale).

# DESIGN IN THE UNIVERSE

The information gathered from the various space probes has confirmed that life is not known on the other planets of the solar system; nor could it exist there, for the prime essentials for life are missing: they all lack oxygen and liquid water. Planet Earth is the only heavenly body in this system that can sustain life. It is unique. This fact should cause one to ask, Why only life on Planet Earth?

## The Creator speaks

Over 2,000 years before space probes were thought of the Creator summarised His creative work in very simple and understandable terms: "I have made the earth, and created man upon it: I, even My hands, have stretched out the heavens, and all their host have I commanded" (Isa. 45:12). That is not boastful language, nor is it typical of the fanciful descriptions of mythology; it is a simple statement of a profound truth. The Creator's claim is easy to read and accept in faith, even though our finite minds cannot comprehend all that is involved in that statement.

In Genesis 22:17 the Almighty God said to Abraham: "I will multiply thy seed as the stars of the heaven, and as the sand which is upon the sea shore". At first glance it might be thought that this is a poor comparison, for the grains of sand are innumerable, while the stars can be counted. But modern astronomical instruments have revealed that there are over a trillion stars out there, invisible even to an ordinary telescope. How many more there may be only the Creator knows. Science is slowly revealing more and more wonders of the universe, and each new discovery confirms the Bible pictures.

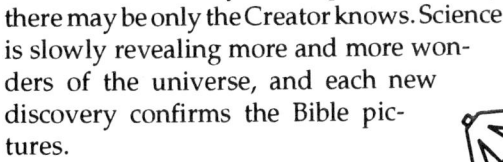

It is the mathematical precision of the universe that has enabled astronomers to calculate the exact time taken by the earth on its annual journey round

A flat table on the back of a giant tortoise—an ancient idea about the earth. But the Bible says that God "hangeth the earth upon nothing".

# DESIGN IN THE UNIVERSE

the sun. (This time is gradually changing and becoming longer. Palaeontologists argue for different days per year in the past.) Unlike the other planets of the solar system, which follow wide elliptical circuits, the earth has a nearly circular circuit. Earth's orbit is unique, yet it is an essential to life. If the earth had a typical planetary circuit of the sun the planet would be alternately baked and frozen, with temperatures that no life could endure. While the earth's range of temperature varies, it suffers none of the extremes that the other planets do. A study of the universe provides superb evidence of design on a vast scale, and of power in control so tremendous that the human mind is unable to measure it. The psalmist expressed the ideal human reaction when he said simply: "The heavens declare the glory of God; and the firmament [expanse] sheweth His handywork" (19:1).

This may be the right place to look at the word 'firmament'. It is not a translation of the Hebrew word but is a result of misunderstanding by the translators of three centuries ago. Men of science at that time regarded the heavens as a sort of dome of firm material through which the stars peeped, and 'firmament' described that concept. But the original Hebrew did not support the idea, and should have been translated 'expanse'.

Other references in the Bible to the universe and the earth show that the Hebrew writers of the Bible were not misled. Even 4,000 years ago it was known that God "hangeth the earth upon nothing" (Job 26:7). Yet for centuries the wise men of the world taught that the earth was a sort of flat table on the back of a giant tortoise, or held up by four monster elephants. The Bible picture of the earth in space was only confirmed scientifically when men took photographs of the earth from the moon. This showed a beautiful blue globe, literally hanging on nothing. While the Bible is not a book of science, its descriptions of nature are not inaccurate.

## References
1. Sir James Jeans (1932), *The Mysterious Universe*, Cambridge University Press, p. 140.
2. Professor Albert Einstein (1940), *The World as I See It*, Watts & Co., London, p. 9.
3. *New Scientist* (16 Nov. 1978), p. 506.
4. *Scientific American* (May 1963), p. 53.

# 5

## EVIDENCE OF DESIGN IN PLANET EARTH

Do you ever wonder what it would be like to travel in space? In fact you already are travelling in space on a well-appointed spacecraft! Planet Earth is travelling at an incredible speed through space on a regular orbit around the sun. You are just one of many millions of passengers on this specifically equipped spacecraft. Have you noticed how carefully everything has been provided for your journey? Dr Morrison, president of the New York Academy of Science, has been quoted as saying that "So many essential conditions are necessary for life to exist on earth, that it is mathematically impossible that all of them could exist in a proper relationship—by chance—on earth, at one time". In other words, Planet Earth's unique conditions for sustaining life could not have been accidental, they must have been purposeful.

What are these essential requirements for life? Most of them we tend to take for granted. The air we breathe is seldom noticed until the atmosphere is polluted, or poor ventilation affects us, or we have congested lungs. Yet the air we breathe is a balanced mixture of gases that is just right for life. The oxygen that is so essential for life is only twenty-one per cent of the atmosphere. If it were much more than this the air would be dangerously combustible; if much less, we should all be fighting for breath like the mountaineers on Mount Everest, where oxygen is rare. Most of the air is composed of the inert gas nitrogen, with tiny traces of other gases. Our air is beautifully balanced to sustain aerobic life. This fact has been highlighted by recent scientific investigation of the other planets.

**MERCURY,** the impossible planet: "*By all accounts, the planet nearest the sun is the wrong size and in the wrong place. It is a planet of extremes, the closest to the sun, travelling fastest and both very hot and very cold. Its climate is not exactly inviting*" (*New Scientist*, 1 June 1991, p. 26). These are good reasons for being thankful that we are on a planet that was purposely designed for life. Let us thank the Creator for this privilege.

●

"**THE HIGH** oxygen content of the Earth's atmosphere sets our planet apart from all other bodies in the Solar System" (*Nature*, 6 September 1990, p. 17). The writer can find no evolutionary answer to this problem. Our essential oxygen is a mystery until we accept the miraculous creation of the earth, and its specific preparation for habitation. How often do we stop to thank God for His careful balancing of the contents of the air we breathe?

●

**THIRTY** prominent cosmologists and astronomers met in Sweden to discuss the origin of the universe. Various theories were aired, from the Big Bang to the 'cold dark matter' theory. The report of the conference concluded: "*Cosmologists, and the rest of us, may have to forgo attempts at understanding the Universe and simply marvel at its infinite complexity and strangeness*" (*Scientific American*, October 1990, p. 74). We can all marvel, and some of us can praise and magnify the Creator for His wonders in both the earth and the heavens, and thank Him for the privilege of allowing us to know Him through His Word and His dear Son.

Their atmosphere has been proved to consist mainly of poisonous gases, while the essential oxygen cannot be detected at all. That is why there is no life there. Planet Earth is unique.

The water that is so essential for life can also be taken for granted. It is only when it is scarce, or badly polluted, that most of us realise its value. Yet the surface of our planet reveals more water than land in the vast oceans that cover two thirds of the planet. Water is a unique substance. It is a combination of two gases, yet it is a liquid. It is an essential ingredient of life, yet it cannot be detected in liquid form on any other planet. Liquid water is unique to Planet Earth.

**Sun and moon**

Although Planet Earth is travelling at about 44,000 miles an hour around the sun, the sun is also moving at a vast speed in space, taking us with it. Our life on earth is dependent on the warmth and energy emitted by the sun. Yet if we were only five per cent nearer to the source of our warmth the heat would be so intense that the planet would become sterile, while if we were only five per cent more distant earth would be in a permanent deep freeze. The precise position of the planet in relation to the sun is a vital factor for life. Of the planets in the solar system, earth is unique in being the only one where life can be sustained. Space probes to the other planets have established that none of them has the essential conditions for life. Even when the astronauts made their historic visit to our neighbour, the moon, they had to take supplies of air and water with them, for these essentials to life are not found on the moon.

Too much . . .    Too Little . . .    Just right!

# DESIGN IN PLANET EARTH 45

The moon has no light of itself; it is a purpose-made reflector of the light of the sun. The men on the moon discovered that its surface is covered with countless millions of little glass beads, which act as reflectors. In this respect the moon is unique. Could it have been accidental that the moon was provided with this feature? In what other ways does the moon affect life on earth? It may not be realised that it is vital to life on earth that the moon should be placed precisely where it is at 240,000 miles away. If it were only 200,000 miles away its effect upon the ocean tides of the earth would be catastrophic. Fifty-foot tidal surges would sweep the coasts; vast areas of land would be uninhabitable. If there was no moon our oceans would be stagnant and putrefying ponds. It is the moon's tidal influence that keeps cleansing currents of water on the move in every ocean all the time.

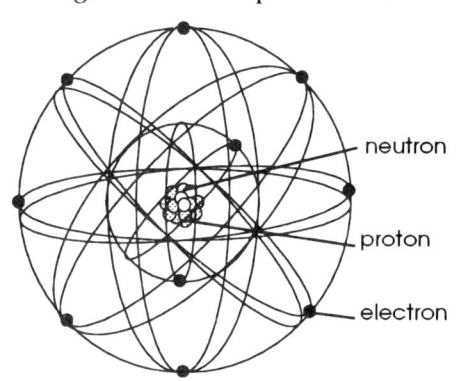

## Earth's elements

The mathematical precision and perfection of creation can be seen in the elements of which our planet is composed. The elements are themselves composed of atoms, each atom being a tiny planetary system of electrons in orbit around a nucleus, in the same pattern as the solar system. Even the air we breathe consists of millions of atoms with every breath.

The structure of a neon atom, atomic number 10

All the elements, although they appear to be so different, consist of various numbers of electrons orbiting around a similar number of protons in the nucleus. For example, the hydrogen atom has one electron orbiting one proton, while the uranium atom has ninety-two electrons orbiting ninety-two protons. Although these elements are so different, the electrons and protons are basically the same in both elements. The scientist Henry Mosely found that there is a precise mathematical order in the elements, based upon the number of orbiting electrons. With this knowledge all known natural elements have been numbered from 1 to 92.

## Natural symmetry

The evidence of order and symmetry in nature is a convincing reason for seeing planet earth as a part of a grand design. The design has been there from the beginning, but only this century has science been able to reveal the precise mathematical precision of the solar system, of the essentials for life on earth, and of the pattern of the elements. However matter was formed in the beginning, however the solar system was put into motion, however the essential conditions for life on earth were organised, it is evident that it was purposeful, that there was a grand design, that it could not have been the result of blind chance or of a stellar accident.

At a meeting of scientists at the University of Maryland in 1979, to discuss what are the essentials for life, it was stated: "No planet outside of the solar system has yet been found, and even if another planetary system is formed, there is no certainty it will produce a solid planet like Earth, which contains nearly 100 elements, including those essential to life".[1]

One evolutionist writer said: "The Judaic, Muslim and Christian traditions all propose a rational deity, who is the Creator of, but distinct from, the physical Universe. This Universe carried the imprint of a rational design in its detailed working. This belief was implicit in the work of Isaac Newton and his contemporaries during the rise of modern science in the 17th century". Then, being an atheist, he wrote: "Although the theistic dimension has long since faded, its implications for the natural order of the physical world remain little changed".[2]

Professor Albert Einstein has written: "Our admiration for Kepler (who discovered the harmony of the orbits of the planets) is transcended only by our admiration and reverence for the mysterious harmony of nature, in which we find ourselves".[3] "The Earth is unique because it is the only world in our Solar System upon which we could survive", wrote Patrick Moore in his *Guide to the Planets*. Lord Kelvin summarised the situation in these words: "Overwhelmingly strong proofs of intelligent and benevolent design lie around us".[4]

Nearly three thousand years ago the wise king said: "When He prepared the heavens, I [Wisdom] was there: when He set a compass upon the face of the depth: when He established the

# DESIGN IN PLANET EARTH 47

*The symmetry of snowflakes is evidence of a grand design.*

clouds above: when He strengthened the fountains of the deep: when He gave to the sea His decree, that the waters should not pass His commandment: when He appointed the foundations of the earth: then I [Wisdom] was by Him . . ." (Prov. 8:27-30).

## References
1. *The New York Times* (4 Nov. 1979), p. 12.
2. *New Scientist* (15 Oct. 1988), p. 58.
3. *Nature* (21 Mar. 1990), p. 285.
4. *Transactions of the Victoria Institute*, No. 124, p. 267.

# 6

# EVIDENCE OF DESIGN IN THE LIVING CELL

All forms of life are composed of living cells. Until quite recently the cell had been thought of as just a 'gob of goo', too simple to be worth looking at carefully. However, with the scientific development of the electron microscope, the cell has now been revealed in its amazing complexity. Even though one living cell is so small that it cannot be seen by the unaided eye, it has now been shown to be a hive of activity in miniature.

"Looking at a living cell through the microscope is a bit like having a bird's eye view of Piccadilly Circus in rush hour. Vesicles and organelles show a complex two-way traffic pattern along intracellular highways of micro-tubules radiating out of the nucleus". Thus wrote a scientist of what he saw within the cell.[1] The adult human body may consist of as many as 100 trillion cells of over thirty different types.[2] Of the many different shapes and sizes of human cells, the largest is the female ovum (from which a new human body may develop), which is one hundredth of an inch across. Within each cell is a system of chemical 'laboratories', in which the building materials of the body are made. Each cell has its own programme of production, of reproduction, of communication, of nutrition, of repair and of waste removal. The energy required by the body is produced in the powerhouse of each cell, the mitochondria. Within the nucleus is a long molecule, up to two yards long, known as the DNA molecule (DNA is the commonly used acronym for deoxyribonucleic acid), which contains a mass of instructions for the working of the cell.

# DESIGN IN THE LIVING CELL

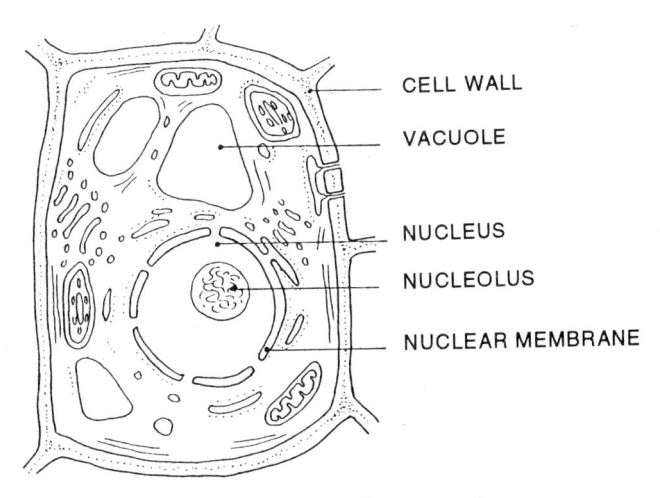

The structure of a plant cell.

One author says of the cell: "The complexity of the simplest known type of cell is so great that it is impossible to accept that such an object could have been thrown together by some kind of freakish, vastly improbable event. Such an occurrence would be indistinguishable from a miracle".[3] More details of the wonders now revealed within the cell are to be found in a book with the title, *A Guided Tour of the Living Cell*. Readers are invited to take three tours of the cell, which are accomplished in 400 pages in two volumes. Such a tour leaves one mightily impressed by the miracle of life in each unseen cell, as revealed by science.[4] It has now been established that some of the working parts of the cell have a life of only a few minutes, yet they are constantly being replaced, unknown to the owner.[5]

Indeed, science is wonderful to be able to reveal and make known some of these hidden wonders of the life that is everywhere around and within us. That such amazing complexities of life could be the result of a chance coming together of stray atoms, or an accident of nature, is quite unthinkable.

**A look at the genetic material**

The genetic material in the simplest cell is exceedingly complex and includes the DNA and RNA (nucleic acids composed of hundreds of nucleotides). Also needed, in order for the information encoded in the genetic material to be used by a cell, are ribosomes (that translate messenger RNA into the amino acid sequences that form proteins), plus at least seventy enzymes and other proteins (which in turn are essential for the translation of the instructions contained in the DNA), plus energy supplies in the form of molecules such as glucose and ATP, and a generous supply of nucleotides and amino acids.

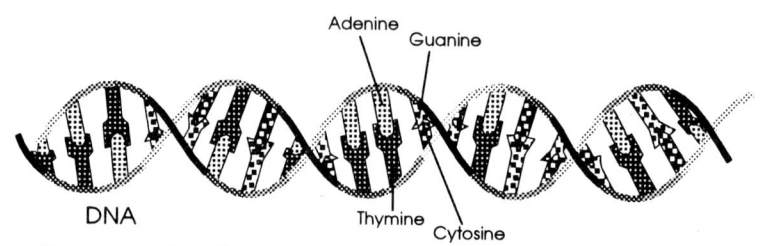

The number of possible 'messages' in a segement of 15 pairs could be over a thousand million combinations

Thus each living cell contains something like an elaborate computer program packed with information and cell organelles for its working and development; yet the information to allow production of many essential components of the genetic coding system is found only in the genetic coding system itself. This raises the question, How did the system originate? It appears to be a continuous circle without an evident beginning, as J. Monod observed.[6] The genetic coding system has been described as "a marvel of detailed and complex architecture".[7] "The origin of the genetic code is the most baffling aspect of the problem of the origin of life".[8]

"Rather than accept the fantastically small probability of life having arisen through the blind forces of nature, it seemed better to suppose that the origin of life was a deliberate intellectual act", wrote Fred Hoyle.[9] "The puzzle surely would have been interpreted as the most powerful sort of evidence for a special creation".[10] "The most elementary type of cell constitutes a 'mechanism' unimaginably more complex than any machine yet thought of, let alone constructed by man".[11] "The human genetic code within each cell of the body may be carrying as many as six billion detailed instructions for the growth and development of the human organism".[12] The vast amount of information within each living cell has

# DESIGN IN THE LIVING CELL 51

been compared to "about a hundred million pages of information in the *Encyclopaedia Britannica*".[13]

Each cell is a hive of activity, where many different chemical processes are taking place, mainly making the building blocks of the body. These are moved to their appointed places according to the instructions contained in the DNA. Thus the bone cells, the very long nerve cells, the transparent lens cells of the eyes and the cells of keratin are directed to their appropriate places. This system may be likened to a building site on which millions of bricks have been delivered, ready to be correctly placed by the builders according to the plans of the architect. Nobody would be so foolish as to assert that the heap of bricks could form a complex building by chance. In a similar way, it is obvious that living cells cannot form even the simplest of living organisms by chance.

### Life's bar code

The uniqueness of each form of life is ensured by the DNA, which can be likened to the bar code of life. It effectively identifies every form of life as separate and distinct from every other form of life. Just as commercial products are now marked with a bar code to give them their own unique identification, so every form of life has the DNA implanted within each cell.

Nobody would be so foolish as to suggest that the commercial bar-code system was caused by an accident in the printing works; nor should the DNA be seen as an accident of nature. The bar-code system has obviously been carefully designed and devised by competent technicians. So how much more obvious it must be that the far more detailed and complex bar code in every cell was designed and devised by a very competent superintelligence, even before life began.

The *Scientific American* had a feature article entitled "High Fidelity of DNA Duplication".[14] It stated: "Generation after generation, through countless cell divisions, the genetic heritage of living things is scrupulously preserved in DNA. Why are so few mistakes made when DNA is copied? Evidence drawn from many different disciplines has revealed that discrete enzymatic processes cooperate to ensure the hi-fi replication of DNA". Thus science is revealing

**NOT SO** long ago a cell was regarded as just a bit of 'goo'. Now science is revealing to some extent how very complicated every living cell is: "*When a cell needs to make a particular protein, something has to 'read' the relevant genes and translate each codon. Then the appropriate amino acid must be found, and all the amino acids must be assembled together in the correct order to make the protein*" ("Inside Science", *New Scientist*, 3 December 1988, p. 2). How does 'something' in the cell 'read' the formula, and then perform all the complex work of assembly, all by its little self?

•

"*HOW DO very similar genes produce very different cells? The elaborate chemical messages that control differentiation are now being deciphered. A human being has more than 250 different types of cells, and each must occupy and function in its proper place. Yet all cells have the same genes encoded in the DNA . . . We're studying what I call the 'brain' of the 'smart gene' . . . this complex is now being seen as a 'sloppy' computer in which the signals are combined to make a decision about whether to switch on the gene*" (*Scientific American*, August 1991, p. 12). Even evolutionists are now seeing a 'computer' within each cell, yet fail to see evidence of the Programmer for the computer. That such intricate information should have evolved by chance is quite incredible, and research such as this should sound the death knell of the theory of evolution.

•

"*LIVING cells are protein factories that are vital for the survival of organisms. Thus, they have elaborate strategies for survival. If environmental stress, such as a chemical or temperature, shuts down their protein-making machinery, cells undertake a series of intricate steps to resume production*" (*Scientific American*, December 1990, p. 32). How little most of us know of the fearfully and wonderfully devised living cells within our bodies! Let us thank our Creator for His amazing gift of life.

# DESIGN IN THE LIVING CELL                53

why the DNA of grass ensures the faithful reproduction of grass, while the DNA of monkeys ensures that their progeny are only monkeys. As so simply and clearly stated in Genesis 1, all forms of life reproduce "after their kind". In other words, the Creator said that there was to be no evolution from one kind to another, and this was, and still is, ensured by the faithfulness of the DNA. While there is a measure of variability within each kind—for no two individuals have identical DNA—yet that variability has strict limits, and no evolution of one kind to another has taken place, nor could take place.

The DNA in each cell is far more complex than may have been gathered from the above description. The DNA molecule, hidden within the nucleus of each cell, is a specific arrangement of only four chemical compounds called nucleotides. Yet they are so arranged as to give very precise information. The words on this page are an arrangement of letters in a precise form to give a message. If the same letters were disarrayed, they would not give the message. Just as the letters have been arranged by an intelligence, so the ordered arrangement of the DNA, with its message for the working of the cell, must have been the product of an intelligence, indeed a superintelligence.

A group of scientists have expressed themselves very clearly on the implications of the scientific discovery of the DNA within each cell. They wrote: "an intelligible communication via radio signal from some distant galaxy would be widely hailed as evidence of an intelligent source. Why then doesn't the message sequence of the DNA molecule also constitute prima facie evidence for an intelligent source? After all, DNA information is not just analogous to a message sequence, such as Morse Code, *it is* such a message sequence".[15] Another scientist expressed himself more forcefully with this comment: "At that moment, when the RNA/DNA system became understood, the debate between evolutionists and creationists should have come to a screeching halt".[16]

The psalmist summarised the situation in very simple non-scientific terms when he wrote: "I will praise Thee; for I am fearfully and wonderfully made: marvellous are Thy works; and that my soul knoweth right well" (139:14). Many centuries after those words were written, science is revealing something of how fearfully and wonderfully we are made. The living cell, with its genetic code, the DNA, hidden within it, must surely be recognised as the blueprint of the Creator within every living cell on earth.

### References
1. *Nature* (12 Nov. 1987), p. 106.
2. *Science Digest* (Sept./Oct. 1980), p. 49.
3. Michael Denton (1985), *A Theory in Crisis*, Adler, p. 264.
4. *New Scientist* (9 May 1985), p. 35.
5. *Nature* (30 Nov. 1989), p. 498.
6. J. Monod (1972), *Chance and Necessity*, Collins, London, p. 143.
7. Carl Sagan (1974), *The Encyclopaedia Britannica*, p. 894.
8. *New Scientist* (15 Apr. 1982), p. 149.
9. *Engineering and Science* (Nov. 1981), p. 8.
10. *American Scientist* (1971), p. 305.
11. Thorpe (1974), *Studies in the Philosophy of Biology*, p. 117.
12. *Science Digest* (Sept./Oct. 1981), p. 32.
13. Carl Sagan (1980), *Cosmos*—a broadcast talk on P.B.S.
14. *Scientific American* (Aug. 1988), p. 24.
15. Thaxton, Bradley & Olsen (1984), *The Mystery of Life's Origin*, Philosophical Library, New York, p. 211.
16. I. L. Cohen (1984), *Darwin Was Wrong—A Study in Probabilities*, New Research Publications, New York.

# 7

# EVIDENCE OF DESIGN IN THE HUMAN BRAIN, EYES AND EARS

From a consideration of the marvels of the living cell in all its complexity, we now turn to the specialised cells that form the human brain, eyes and ears.

## The brain

Without going into a biological study of the actual structure of the brain, it will be enough for this study to enumerate some of the amazing capabilities of the brain. "In man is a three-pound brain which, as far as we know, is the most complex and orderly arrangement of matter in the Universe", wrote Dr Isaac Asimov.[1] Another scientist, Dr Loren Eiseley, described the brain as the "most miraculous creation in the world", even though he is an evolutionist who does not believe in either miracles or creation.

What makes it so special? Even when the body is asleep, and the brain appears to be at rest, yet it is in control of such bodily functions as breathing, digestion, blood circulation, growth, elimination and the nervous system. When the brain is conscious its range of activities is almost too vast to enumerate. Sight, hearing, touch, smell and muscular movements have their centre in the brain. The brain is connected to every part of the body by nerve cells, which transmit messages by electrochemical impulses at fantastic speeds for the brain to evaluate and act upon.

Even more amazing is the ability to retain information and then to recall that information. Beyond our understanding is the ability to imagine, to think out problems, to interpret information. Even beyond this is consciousness, our awareness of immaterial and abstract concepts such as beauty, love, loyalty, faithfulness and obedience. The origin of man's consciousness is quite unknown to science.

The brain structure consists of about 10,000 million neurons, powered by ten times as many glia cells (biological batteries). Each of the neurons may have hundreds of thousands of nerve connections. Passing between them all the time is information that makes the brain an exceedingly busy communication system handling possibly a hundred million messages every second. This all requires energy. But, unlike the communication systems of man's invention, the brain is exceedingly economical in its use of energy. Oxygen is the vital ingredient of the brain's power supply, and one quarter of the body's oxygen is used by the brain, conveyed there by the blood stream. Thus fresh air helps to keep the brain clear.

Whole books have been written on the detailed working of the brain, yet there is much that is not yet understood. What is clear

# THE HUMAN BRAIN, EYES AND EARS   57

is that our brain is marvellous evidence of purposeful design and construction. So complex a structure performing such a vast range of activities could not conceivably be the result of a "fortuitous concourse of atoms", any more than an international telephone exchange could be the product of an accident in a scrap metal yard. The miracle of the human brain is good evidence that it was designed and perfected by a superintelligence. It is much too easy to take the miracle of the grey matter in our skull for granted, without considering that it is shouting out loud that the Creator formed it, and gave it to man to use in the Creator's honour.

## The eye

Just as the brain is composed of many different types of cell, all placed in position for their part in the total activity, so the eye is composed of many different types of cell, each carefully placed to complete the organ of sight. If the transparent cells of the lens were to be placed in the retina there would be no sight. If the optic nerve was misplaced there would be no sight. Thus it must be obvious that the eye has been carefully and purposefully designed and constructed.

Science has imitated the eye by producing the camera. But unless we had eyes to see the picture the camera would be useless. The microscope and the telescope reveal much that the unaided eye cannot see, but they would be useless unless we had eyes to see what they reveal. Our eyes are not cameras, although they have lenses. To make a lens for a camera or a telescope is the task of very highly skilled technicians, using specially designed equipment and great care. But the lens of the eye was not made that way. It was formed by specialist cells that were put into place very early in the growth of the body. Could it have been by chance that the right kind of cells were put in the right place to make a seeing eye?

Science has revealed something of the complexity of the eye. The lens gathers light and projects an image onto the retina, which consists of many millions of delicate photoreceptors called rods and cones. From these many thousands of nerve fibres convey the picture to the brain. Then the brain interprets what has been seen. That is a much too simplified version of the miracle of sight, but it illustrates the great complexity of the visual system, many details

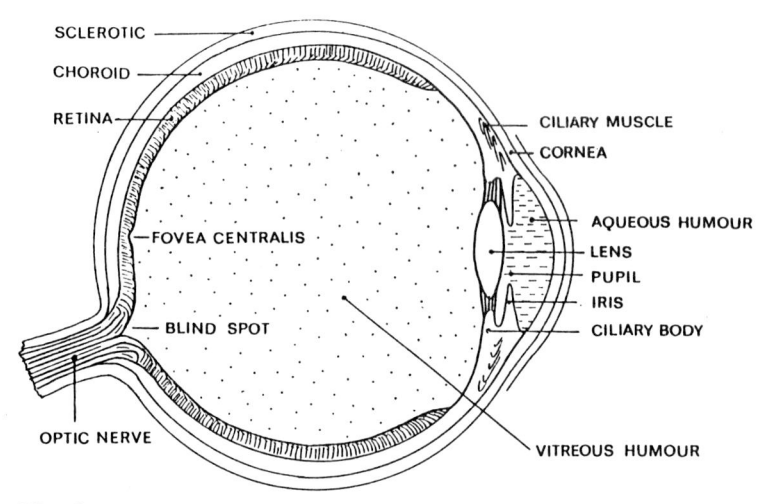

**The human eye**

of which are not yet understood by science. It is no wonder that Sir Isaac Newton, the world-famous pioneer scientist, wrote: "Was the eye contrived without skill in opticks, and the ear without knowledge of sound?".[2] Even Charles Darwin had to admit: "That the eye, with all its inimitable contrivances, could have been formed by natural selection, seems, I freely confess, absurd in the highest degree".[3]

To these comments by men of science it seems appropriate to add the very pointed comment of the Creator, found in Psalm 94:8,9: "Understand, ye brutish among the people: and ye fools, when will ye be wise? He that planted the ear, shall He not hear? He that formed the eye, shall He not see?". On the same subject the wise man wrote: "The hearing ear, and the seeing eye, the LORD hath made even both of them" (Prov. 20:12). It should be unnecessary to point out that, unless all parts of the visual system were put together in the right way and at the same time, there would be no sight. Yet the world of nature has millions of creatures with sight; ten different visual systems have been noticed, some even more complex than human sight. Two examples are particularly extraordinary: a spider with eight eyes, and a dragonfly with thousands of facets to each eye. Is it conceivable that these evolved?

## THE HUMAN BRAIN, EYES AND EARS

### The ear

"The hearing ear" is much more than the visible part on each side of the head; the vital part of the ear is hidden within. Sound is transmitted by vibrations in the air. These are received by the eardrum, which passes the sound waves to the 'hammer', from this to the 'anvil', thence to the 'stirrup'. From these tiny bones in the ear the message is converted into electrical impulses involving thousands of highly sensitive hair cells, each receiving its own wavelength. Then the auditory nerve takes the message to the brain. It is through this miniature receiving set, no bigger than a marble, that we hear. The receiving set of smaller creatures is comparably more miniaturised, yet they have acute hearing.

But the ears are for more than hearing. The sense of balance, the movements of the head, consciousness of gravity, and the movements of the body are all detected by this tiny apparatus. Surely it is obvious that so compact and beautifully designed a system could not have evolved a bit at a time until it was complete. The individual separate parts would all have been useless until assembled in the right way.

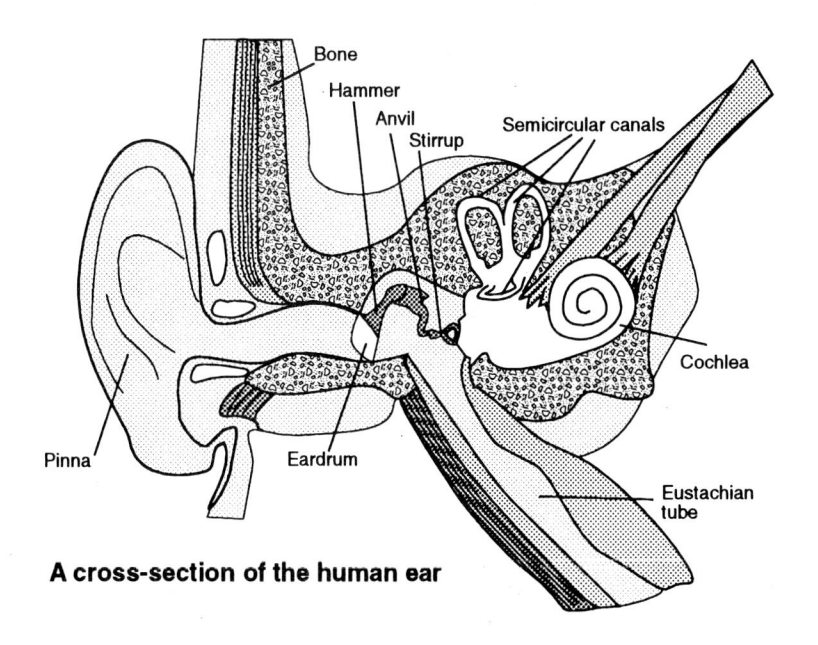

**A cross-section of the human ear**

The evidence of design in these vital parts of the human body should be obvious to any thoughtful person. Science has revealed many details of the human brain, the eye and the ear that were unknown to earlier generations, but is still mystified by some features of these organs. To assume that they just came, we know not how, by chance, is not a logical attitude, nor is it reasonable, nor is it scientific.

Science is based on facts; and the facts about such complex organs as these all point unmistakably to a supernatural and superhuman origin, employing a superintelligence and superskill. Indeed, the full instructions for the making of these complex parts of the body are enshrined in the genetic code, which should be seen as the Creator's blueprint for life. Every cell of every form of life carries the blueprint, which is inexplicable to the evolutionist, but very meaningful to the creationist.

**References**
1. *The Smithsonian* (June 1970), p. 10.
2. Isaac Newton (1704), *Opticks*, New York reprint, p. 369.
3. C. Darwin (1859), *Origin of Species*, Watts & Co., London, p. 167.

# 8

## EVIDENCE OF DESIGN IN BEES, ANTS AND SPIDERS

It would be easy to enjoy a taste of honey without giving thought to the bees that produce it. Honey is a concentration of sweet nectar that has been gathered by honey bees from various kinds of flowers. The bees' objective in gathering and storing honey is to provide food for themselves during the winter. They store the honey in cells made of beeswax—the honeycomb. The wax is manufactured by the bees from honey, which is processed within the body of the bee and then exuded in small flakes. The wax is then formed into perfectly uniform six-sided cells, a most economical method of construction.

The ingenuity shown by bees in seeking and finding the sources of nectar, in concentrating it into honey, in preparing storage cells, in packing and sealing their food supply, is all evidence of a very purposeful life style. These busy insects have an amazing instinct for organising their activities for the self-preservation of the colony.

But their ingenuity does not end there. Because they all work for the benefit of one another, and for following generations, they are referred to as social insects. Each colony has three types of bees: the queen, the drones and the workers. The queen, which can live up to five years, spends most of her life within the hive. She leaves it at the start of her life as an adult on mating flights, and will only leave it again if the colony swarms. Her principal function is to lay eggs. Under suitable conditions from March to July she will lay 1,500 eggs per day. These will hatch to produce the succeeding generations of bees. Worker bees attend to her every need. Queens and drones (the male bees) are the reproductive members of the colony. There is usually only one queen and, in the summer, a few hundred drones which live for a few months at the most.

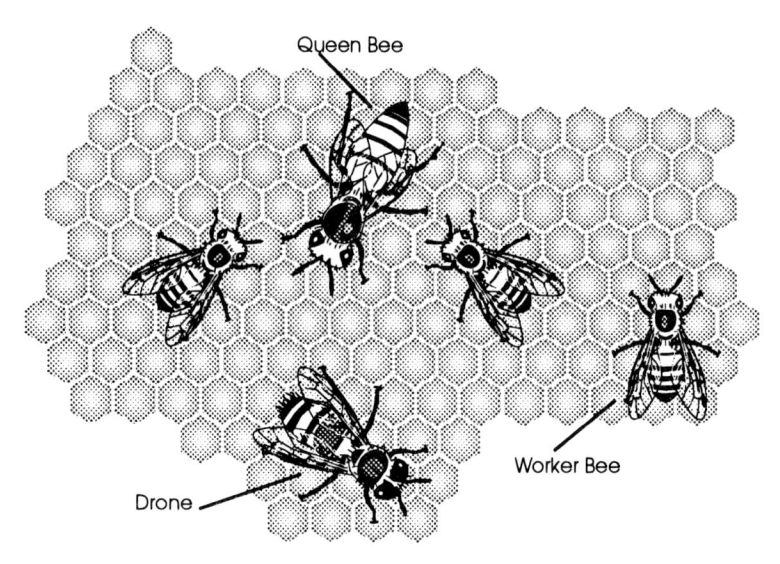

**The workers**

Worker bees are non-reproductive females. They live about three to four weeks in the summer, but six to seven months in the winter. A moderate colony will contain about 50,000 workers. They have a wide range of duties and are equipped with special glands, not present in queens or drones, that enable them to produce special food for the grubs and the wax used for building the comb.

Besides attending to the queen they feed the emerging grubs, keep the hive clean, guard it from intruders (such as wasps), provide air conditioning, convert honey into wax, build the comb, and forage around the hive for sources of nectar, gathering pollen and nectar for storage. They even communicate information to one another about the sources of nectar by means of the bee 'dance'.

Is it conceivable that the bees themselves, with a brain the size of a pinhead, could have thought out all the details of this beautifully organised lifestyle, this ideal insect society? It is clear that their

"**FOSSILS** in northeast Spain show that spiders spun webs to catch their prey at least 138 million years ago. The fossil spiders look as if they are still made of the original spider's cuticle . . . scientists can see fine details such as bristles on the hairs of the spiders' legs . . . and tarsal claws. Modern spiders that spin webs display just this pattern of claws" (*New Scientist*, 16 September 1989, p. 32). What the scientists seem unable to see is that the spiders have not evolved in all those years! This puzzles the evolutionists, but is satisfying to one who believes in Divine creation.

●

"**NOTHING** can beat an insect for aerial acrobatics. A fly, for example, can loop the loop, hover, reverse direction and land upside down, all in a fraction of a second. It owes that agility to ribbed wings that are subtly engineered, flexible aerofoils. Insect wings have few, if any technological parallels, yet . . . Subtle details of engineering and design, which no man-made aerofoil can match, reveal how insect wings are remarkably adapted to the aerobatics of flight" (*Scientific American*, November 1990, p. 66). Evidence of subtle engineering and design is not the language of evolution, which relies on random changes for development. Every one of the half-million kinds of insects that fly has a fully perfected flight system, and has had it from the beginning, as proved by the discovery of fossil insects.

●

"**CATERPILLARS** come in a bewildering variety of shapes and sizes—more than 100,000 species worldwide . . . [they] can increase in weight by as much as 2,000 times" (*New Scientist*, 23 February 1991, p. 52). Even more amazing is that they are a stage on the way to becoming winged insects of one kind or another—what might be termed a 'designed evolution', but certainly not an 'accident of nature'.

instinct is transmitted by the genetic code, and passed on in the code from generation to generation. As has been pointed out, the genetic code is far too complex to have been the product of chance, but is evidence of a superintelligence that implanted the complex information in that code: the Creator.

Whether bees know it or not, they also provide a very essential service to the flowers that they visit when seeking for nectar. In the act of gathering nectar the bees transfer male pollen from the stamen of the flower to the female stigma of another flower, thereby cross-fertilising the flowers. This is the first stage in seed formation. The bee's body would appear to have been designed for this very purpose. While its mouth and hairy tongue are perfect tools for gathering the nectar, its legs have 'baskets' for the storage of pollen as it flits from flower to flower.

Although this brief description is a simplification of the abilities and activities of the honey bee, it is enough to demonstrate that they were designed the way they are from the beginning, or there would now be no bees to tell the tale. The occasional discovery of a bee enshrined in transparent amber, preserved intact from prehistoric times, proves that bees are the same now as they were then, and have not evolved.

### The ants

Ants also are known as social insects, because they work together as a community. Although there are many different kinds of ants, most of them have certain features in common. The males are winged; the females are only winged until they have mated, after which they spend the rest of their lives in the nest, laying eggs. Most of the colony are wingless workers. Their or-

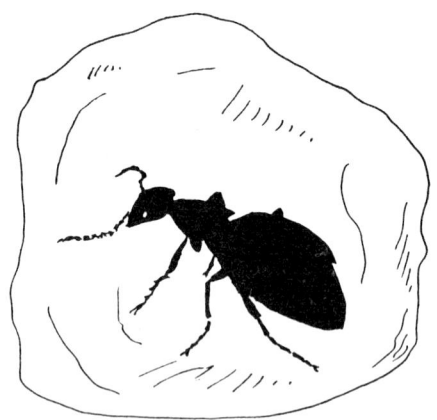

Drawing of an ant in amber. Thousands of examples in museums show that insects are still as they were long ago.

ganisation of labour is as remarkable as that of the honey bees, yet it is different.

The workers gather food, make the nest, and in some species dig tunnels. Nests vary from a pile of forest debris or pine needles to a skilfully made nest of leaves sewn together. Some species of ants keep herds of aphids, milking them for food. Other species have underground gardens of fungus for food. Army ants have no permanent nest, but bivouac where they are as they move from place to place. Desert ants can steer a straight course across featureless sand dunes, probably using solar navigation techniques. Ants have been known to make bridges over water by sacrificing themselves to form a chain of interlocked dead bodies. The many abilities and activities of ants have filled many a book.

Their instinctive way of life and their physical structure have not changed over the centuries, as is proved by the thousands of ants that have been found preserved in amber, some of them in the act of milking an aphid. There is no valid reason to think that they have ever evolved. The evidence is that they were provided with a genetic code by their Creator, and have continued in a similar way of life from that day to this.

### Spiders

The spider is not an insect, for it has eight legs instead of six, and several other unique features. Most spiders have the ability to spin threads of silk, and many of them can weave the thread into intricate webs to catch flies and moths. Spiders' silk is made of processed flies.

Many spiders can produce more than one type of silk. There is a type of spider silk that is stronger than a comparable thread of steel. Some silk is elastic, and some is sticky. The *Araneus* spiders can spin various types of silk to build their webs because they have six different types of silk glands. The webs of silk are made in many different patterns, each species of spider having its own shape. They are all designed as flytraps, yet the spider does not get trapped itself, for it can oil its feet so that the sticky silk is ineffective. Some varieties of baby spiders spin a length of very fine light silk that acts as a kite in the wind and takes the infant to pastures new.

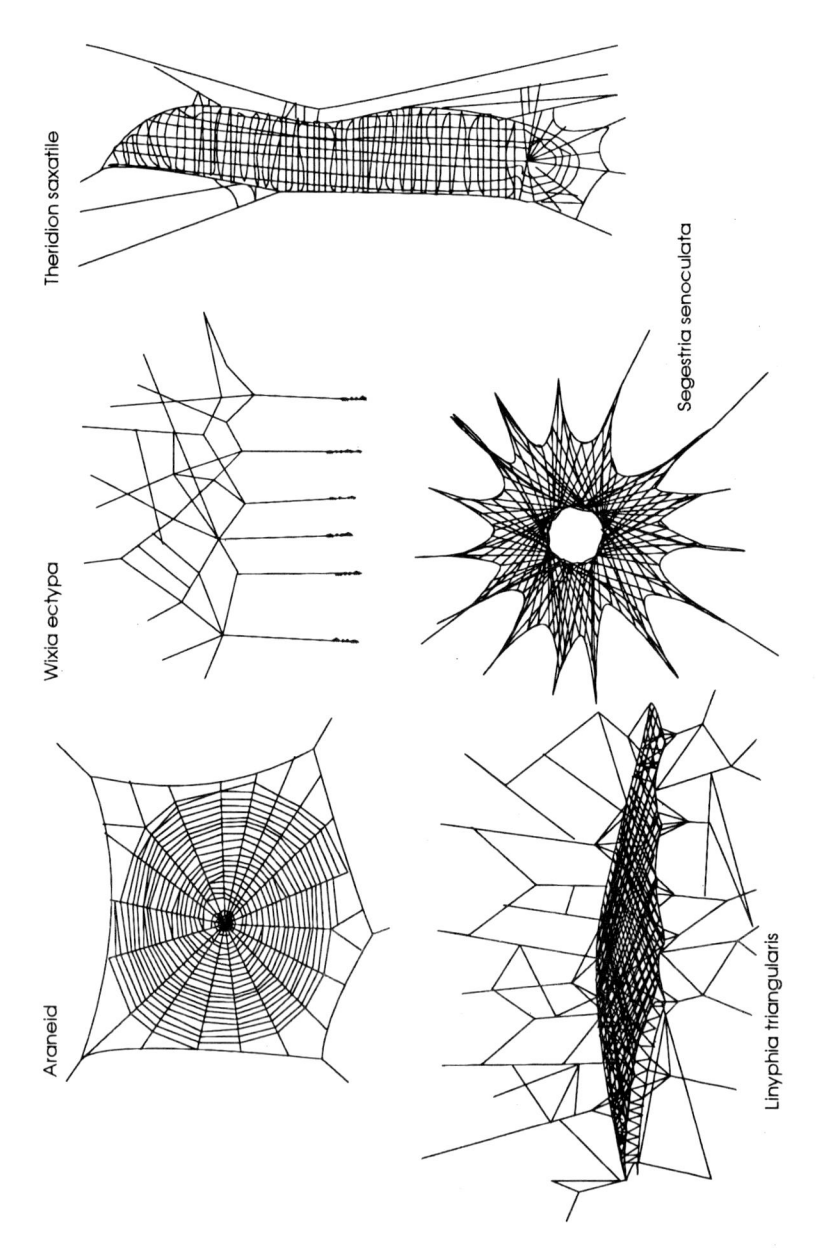

Different types of spiders' webs.

Perfectly formed spiders have been found in fossils, as well as in transparent amber. They can be seen to be complete in every detail of their complex bodies, thus proving that spiders are not evolving, but are still just as they were in prehistoric times. For example, the *New Scientist* reported that "Palaeontologists [scientists who study fossils] have found fossils in North East Spain which show that spiders spun webs to catch their prey at least 138 million years ago ... The unique feature of the fossil spiders is that they have tarsal claws ... Spiders use these claws specifically to handle thread and weave it into webs ... modern spiders that spin webs display just this pattern of claws".[1]

There is no evidence whatever that spiders have ever been anything but spiders. Their instinctive skills to obtain food and protect themselves must have been present from the beginning, or there would be no spiders. There is evidence of the Creator's detailed design in every aspect of the life style of the spider. No spider could have survived without its unique innate skills.

**Reference**
1. *New Scientist* (16 Sept. 1987), p. 32.

# 9

# THE GOOD NEWS AT CREATION

Here we are, living on Planet Earth! It is agreed on all sides that life must have had a beginning. It is evident that every form of life seeks to avoid a cessation of life. This natural instinct for self-preservation, so universally true, suggests that all living things regard life as worth living and, indeed, as worth perpetuating.

The first good news for the planet was therefore that a lifeless ball in space was filled with life in over ten million diverse forms, all forming an ecologically balanced unit. The giver of life was the Creator, Who was to reveal Himself as the living God. It is only because the Creator is the living God that He could give life to His creation. This is fully in accord with the scientific law that life can only proceed from previous life, the Law of Biogenesis. This law of nature has always been true, and still is, as every biologist and zoologist can testify. Thus the creation was in accord with scientifically established truth. When creation was completed the Creator pronounced His approval by calling it "very good".

"In the beginning God created". Without these first words of the Bible nothing else would make sense. The good news of how life began is told in easily understood language in the first chapter of Genesis, which also tells how all the needs for life on earth were provided for. Scientific space exploration has now proved that Planet Earth is unique in the solar system, and that its cargo of life is unique. Earth and its variety of life clearly demonstrate the handiwork of a superb Designer, an exceedingly competent Creator, Who is also a caring and loving Sustainer. To suppose, as some do, that these millions of intricately formed living things on earth were the result of countless beneficial accidents of nature is neither reasonable nor scientific, nor statistically possible.

### The love of God in creation

The precision of creation is living proof that the Creator loves life. The elaborate care that the Creator took to prepare the planet to receive life is good evidence that His love for life was practical and 'down to earth'. The preparation of the lifeless planet so that it was capable of accepting and maintaining life is too often taken for granted.

The precision of the relationship between Planet Earth and the sun was no accident. The sun is the source of power, light and heat, as it is for other planets; but the earth is so placed that these are in the right proportions for life. The unique atmosphere that surrounds the earth, with its vital proportion of oxygen, and the unique system of evaporation, circulation and condensation of the vital liquid water, to say nothing of the wide distribution of the essential mineral elements required by life, all point to a purposeful preparation of the planet. The fact that all these necessary conditions were present on earth before life was created is quite impossible to explain by the lottery of chance. It is manifest that the planet was designed and prepared for life in such detail that creation could not be explained as an accidental coming together of atoms. On a purely material basis, the fact of life was good news at creation, and was evidence of the Creator's practical love and care.

One of the men who went to the moon, looking back at the earth, wrote: "That beautiful, warm, living object looked so fragile, so delicate, that if you touched it with a finger it would crumble and fall apart. Seeing this has to change a man, has to make a man appreciate the creation of God and the love of God".[1] Another of the moon explorers wrote of his thoughts as he ascended from the earth: "For the first time in my life I saw the horizon as a curved line. It was accentuated by a thin seam of dark blue light—our atmosphere. Obviously this wasn't the ocean of air I had been told it was. I was terrified by its fragile appearance".[2]

### Meditations about Planet Earth when seen from above by spacemen

"**WHEN** we look into the sky, it seems to us to be endless. We breathe without thinking about it, as is natural. We think without consideration about the boundless ocean of air, and then you sit aboard a space craft, you tear away from earth and within ten minutes you have been carried straight through the layer of air, and beyond there is nothing. Beyond the air there is only emptiness, coldness, darkness. The 'boundless' blue sky, the oceans which give us breath and protect us from the endless black death, is but an infinitesimally thin film. How dangerous it is to threaten even the smallest part of this gossamer covering, this conserver of life" (Vladimir Shatalov).

"**BEFORE** if flew I was already aware of how small and vulnerable our planet is, but only when I saw it from space, in all its ineffable beauty and fragility, did I realise that humankind's most urgent task is to cherish it and preserve it for future generations" (Sigmund Jahn).

"**FOR** those who have seen the earth from space . . . the experience most certainly changes your perspective. The things that we share in our world are far more valuable than those which divide us" (Donald Williams).

"**FROM** space I saw earth—indescribably beautiful, with the scars of national boundaries gone" (Muhammad Ahmad Faris).

"**I WOULD** look at the earth as it would be gliding underneath me and think—How everlasting all this is. After I am gone, and my children and my grandchildren, our earth will still be gliding through the eternity of space in its measured unhurried way" (Vladimir Solovyov).

"**A CHINESE** tale tells of some men sent to harm a young girl, who, upon seeing her beauty, became her protectors rather than her violators. That's how I felt seeing the earth for the first time. I could not help but love and cherish her" (Taylor Wang).

"**NOW I** know why I am here, not for a closer look at the moon, but to look back at our home, the earth" (Alfred Worden).

# THE GOOD NEWS AT CREATION 71

The picture of Planet Earth and its life is that of a purpose-made home for countless forms of life, carefully provided by an indescribably capable and loving Creator. It is not a picture of an accident in space, nor one of having been kicked off by an impersonal 'First Cause', who began life in some elementary form and then left it to develop.

**The love of God for life**

The evidence of the Creator's love and care does not end with creation. When, after the earth had been filled with countless forms of life, man and woman were formed, the Creator gave them instructions. They were entrusted with dominion over all other forms of life. They were instructed what to eat and what to avoid. As a parent warns a child not to touch fire lest he be burned, so the Creator warned man not to eat the fruit of a certain tree. Surely this was evidence of care and love.

Even after the man and woman had ignored the warning, the love of God was still in evidence. He provided for them a covering for their sin, in a form that was a foreshadowing of the way in which the Creator would ultimately provide for the forgiveness of sin by the sacrifice of Jesus, "the Lamb of God"—the final proof that God loves His world. Even that was not the limit of the Creator's love for man. Within the enigmatic pronouncement to the serpent there was hidden a message of hope and love for Eve, that her seed would eventually overcome evil. Although the expulsion of the first pair from the garden in Eden might seem to be a disaster, it was in fact a loving action. It was to ensure that the man and woman did not become immortal sinners, which would have been a most unhappy prospect for them and their Creator.

In spite of man's folly, seen all over the planet in a thousand ways, the Creator has endowed man with many unique abilities and qualities which separate him from all the rest of creation. These abilities can all be used in either of two ways. They can be used to try to reflect some of the love shown to man by his Creator, or they can be used as a means of showing love for self. Yet further evidence of the Creator's love for mankind is to be seen in his comprehensive 'Creator's Guide Book for Life on Earth', more usually known as the Bible. In this His loving purpose for man is revealed, but only to those who use their abilities to seek for it.

To the Greek intellectuals, whose philosophy taught that life sprang by spontaneous generation out of mud, the Apostle Paul pointed out that God "giveth to all life, and breath, and all things" (Acts 17:25). A reminder of this truth is necessary for every new generation, for the love of the Creator and Provider is too often taken for granted, or even denied.

### The good news of the Creator's purpose

Was creation merely a whim of the Creator? Could creation have been an accidental spilling of life without plan or purpose? The evidence, already looked at, that the planet was carefully made ready for the reception of life, indicates that creation was not an accident, nor a mere "chance concourse of atoms", as some allege. "For since the creation of the world God's invisible qualities—His eternal power and divine nature—have been clearly seen, being understood from what has been made, so that men are without any excuse". So wrote the Apostle Paul (Rom. 1:20, NIV), and this observation is even more true today, when science has revealed so much more of the inner wonders of life.

So what is the purpose of it all? One of man's unique abilities is that he can both give and receive detailed communications. The Creator has communicated with man in a number of ways, not the least being the Bible, written by Divinely inspired men. It is in the Bible that the answer to this question is provided. "As truly as I live, all the earth shall be filled with the glory of the LORD" (Num. 14:21), is as concise a statement of the Creator's purpose as one could wish for. This beautiful planet, with all its wonderful variety of life, was created to reflect something of the majesty, the power, the character and the love of its Creator. The Creator spoke through His prophet Isaiah, saying: "thus saith the LORD that created the heavens; God Himself that formed the earth and made it; He hath established it, He created it not in vain, He formed it to be inhabited: I am the LORD; and there is none else" (Isa. 45:18).

Whilst creation was pronounced "very good" by the Creator, that is not the same as saying it was perfect. To achieve a state of perfection necessitates a process of being perfected, and the present order of things on earth is the preparation for a final perfection. In spite of man's rebellion against his Creator, his denial of the existence of a Creator, his pollution of the earth, his rape of its assets and his poisoning of men's minds, nevertheless the Creator has revealed that ultimately it will be possible for His creation to say: "Thou art worthy, O Lord, to receive glory and honour and power: for Thou hast created all things, and for Thy pleasure they are and were created" (Rev. 4:11).

How could such an outcome of the Creator's purpose be achieved? The Creator loves life so much that He is "not willing that any should perish, but that all should come to repentance" (2 Pet. 3:9). For real life to be granted by a loving Creator, man has to change his attitudes. Jesus expressed the change as: "Ye must be born again" (Jno. 3:7).

### The good news of the New Creation

To be born again implies the need for a fresh start for life, in which Jesus is "the way, the truth, and the life". He was the first man of the New Creation, leading the way for others to become "children of the living God" (Rom. 9:26). "Therefore if any man be in Christ, he is a new creature: old things are passed away" (2 Cor. 5:17); "created in Christ Jesus unto good works" (Eph. 2:10); "put on the new man, which after God is created in righteousness and true holiness" (Eph. 4:24).

The New Creation in Jesus Christ looks forward to "new heavens and a new earth, wherein dwelleth righteousness" (2 Pet. 3:13), as foretold by God's prophet Isaiah: "Behold, I create new heavens and a new earth: and the former shall not be remembered" (Isa. 65:17); "For as the new heavens and the new earth, which I will make, shall remain before Me, saith the LORD, so shall your seed and your name remain" (66:22). This is clearly a Divine promise of a new life in a permanent new earth unsullied by man's disobedience, selfishness and violence. This good news of the Creator's purpose to create a New Creation is the good news that Jesus preached, the gospel. Jesus called it the Kingdom of God, or Kingdom of heaven, as distinct from the kingdom of men, as at present. He taught his followers to pray for it, when the will of the

Creator will be done on earth as it is in heaven (Mt. 6:10). The New Creation will live on this Planet Earth, made new. This has always been the Creator's purpose for the earth, for "He formed it to be inhabited" (Isa. 45:18).

The New Creation is of men and women who follow the way shown by Jesus, and who will share the quality of life that Jesus now enjoys, real life without end. The new creatures in Christ Jesus will fill the new earth and render to the Creator the honour, praise and glory that is due to Him. Only then will the Creator's grand design come to fruition, and His purpose in creation be finally accomplished in perfection.

**The tree of life**

The love of the Creator for man and woman is evident from the fact that the tree of life was within man's reach from his creation. It shows that the Creator had a quality of life prepared for man far beyond that with which he had been created. Man's folly put that kind of life out of reach. Yet, in His love for man, a different route to the tree of life was provided. Jesus showed the way, and by his sacrifice for sin made it possible for sinful man to overcome his natural tendencies and receive the promise: "To him that overcometh will I give to eat of the tree of life, which is in the midst of the paradise of God" (Rev. 2:7).

It is the desire and intention of the Creator to fill the earth with life, "For God so loved the world, that He gave His only begotten Son, that whosoever believeth in him should not perish, but have everlasting life. For God sent not His Son into the world to condemn the world; but that the world through him might be saved" (Jno. 3:16,17). The Apostle Paul expresses this truth in easily understood words: "the wages of sin is death; but the gift of God is eternal life through Jesus Christ our Lord" (Rom. 6:23).

The Creator is the sole source of life, with the power to give and to take away. No living creature has a right to life. Life is a gift of the Creator. The fact that the Creator is ready and willing to share life, on certain conditions, is a wonderful testimony to His love for life. "This is life eternal, that they might know Thee the only true God, and Jesus Christ, whom Thou hast sent" (Jno. 17:3). This is more than a recognition of the Creator of the present creation; it is also a recognition of the New Creation as led by Jesus Christ, the "last Adam" and the first-born of the new creatures."

**References**
1. James Irwin, U.S. astronaut (1988), *The Home Planet*, Guild Publishing.
2. Ulf Marbold, *Ibid.*

*The heavens are the LORD's, but the earth hath He given to the children of men"* (Ps. 115:16).

*"Thus saith the LORD that created the heavens; God Himself that formed the earth and made it; He hath established it, He created it not in vain, He formed it to be inhabited; I am the LORD and there is none else. I have not spoken in secret . . ."* (Isa. 45:18).

*"As truly as I live, all the earth shall be filled with the glory of the LORD"* (Num. 14:21).

*"Behold, the righteous shall be recompensed in the earth . . ."* (Prov. 11:31).

*"Those that wait upon the LORD, they shall inherit the earth . . . The righteous shall inherit the land and dwell therein for ever"* (Ps. 37:9,29).

*"Blessed are the meek, for they shall inherit the earth"* (Mt. 5:5).

*"Wherefore be sober and hope to the end for the grace that is to be brought unto you at the revelation of Jesus Christ"* (1 Pet. 1:13).

*"The gift of God is eternal life through Jesus Christ our Lord"* (Rom. 6:23).

# IS EVOLUTION
# A SCIENCE?

# 1

## SCIENCE AND EVOLUTION

What is science? The word comes from the Latin *scio*, meaning to know, or to understand. Hence, strictly speaking, science is knowledge, or something that is definitely known. Dr Karl Popper, famous scientist, in the Medawar Lecture to the Royal Society for the Advancement of Science in 1986 said: "Scientists begin by formulating hypotheses and then proceed to test them by observation . . . if the hypothesis turns out to be inadequate, scientists formulate a new and improved one that can be again subjected to experimental tests".[1] One of these scientific hypotheses is the theory of evolution, or rather, the many theories of evolution, for the writer has counted over fifty theories, all different. Have any of these been tested by observation? Have any of them been repeated experimentally? Have any of them been proved to be a fact of science, as so often claimed?

What is the theory of evolution? It has been defined in this way: "Evolution is a scientific theory proposing that higher forms of life have descended from lower ones".[2] In an article, "The Origin of Darwinism", C. D. Darlington wrote: "Darwinism began as a theory that evolution could be explained by natural selection, and ended as a theory that evolution could be explained as you would like it to be explained".[3] In keeping with this observation, in an article entitled "Bones of Contention" we read: "Scientists are emotional human beings, who carry with them a generous dose of subjectivity into the supposedly objective search for the truth".[4] It is quite possible, therefore, for a scientist to see only what he wants to see, depending on his presuppositions.

There are a number of branches of natural science, such as biology, geology, palaeontology and astronomy. Each of these disciplines has its own specialists, and many universities have a chair for each branch of natural science, with a professor in charge. It is noteworthy that no university in the world offers a degree course in evolution. It is not regarded as a science in itself. But that is not to say that the theory is not professed by any professor. Yet the theory is a long way from being an exact science, and is plagued by an amazing amount of disagreement as to whether, or how, or when, or if, evolution is supposed to have occurred. Why, then, is it assumed to be a scientific fact for purposes of teaching children at school, and students at university, as they study biology, zoology and geology?

### Critics of evolution

Before the time of Darwin and his theory of evolution the idea of a materialistic origin of life had been voiced by a number of philosophers. In response to such theories Sir Isaac

Charles Darwin

Newton, who is regarded as the father of science, wrote: "All material things seem to have been composed ... by the counsel of an Intelligent Agent. For it became Him who created them to set them in order. And, if He did so, it is unphilosophical to seek for any origin of the world, or to pretend that it might arise out of a chance by the mere laws of nature".[5]

From Darwin's day onwards there was scientific opposition to his theory on the grounds that it was not really scientific. Darwin had flown in the face of all received doctrines of natural history and had engaged in uncontrolled speculation. His *Origin of Species* is full of expressions such as "if this", or "suppose that". Many of his contemporaries held that a theory must be tested and proved before it could be accepted as scientific knowledge.

A highly esteemed zoologist at Harvard University, Professor Louis Agassiz, whose writings were well known to Darwin, wrote in 1860: "Darwinism is a scientific mistake, untrue in its facts, unscientific in its methods and mischievous in its tendency". This professor is described thus in *The Encyclopaedia Britannica*: "As a teacher of science, he was extraordinarily skilful, certainly the ablest America has ever known". In more recent times a number of books very critical of Darwinism have appeared, mostly written by evolutionists who have their pet theory to put forward. "For well over 100 years, many biologists have been genuinely unhappy with evolution by natural selection, or Darwinism".[6]

That Darwin had nagging doubts about his own theory soon becomes obvious from reading his own writings. For example: "As by this theory, innumerable transitional forms must have existed. Why do we not find them embedded in the crust of the earth? Why is not all nature in confusion, instead of being, as we see them, well defined species?"[7]

A group of twenty-two biologists who work at the British Museum of Natural History wrote to *Nature* as follows: ". . . we have no absolute proof of the theory of evolution . . . and the theory of evolution would be abandoned tomorrow if a better theory appeared".[8] In the same issue the editor of *Nature* asked: "Is Darwin's theory of evolution a fact, a pack of lies, or something in between?".[9] The fact that the theory has not been scientifically established, in spite of over a century of scientific investigation and the expenditure of vast sums to try to establish it, should be ample evidence that evolution cannot be claimed as a scientific fact.

The pro-evolutionary magazine *Nature*, commenting on the disturbed state of the theory, had an article entitled "Improving on Darwin": "Evolutionary theory continues to be characterised by sharp dissent and often acrimonious debate. Since its birth in the 1850s, the subject has been for the most part a battleground . . . the repeated calls for a 'new paradigm' are the least prepossessing features".[10]

### Is it a modern myth?

The 1956 edition of *Origin of Species* had an introduction by the noted geologist Dr W. R. Thompson. He wrote: "I am not satisfied that Darwin proved his point, or that his influence on scientific and public thinking has been beneficial". Then he commented: "The success of Darwinism was accompanied by a decline in scientific integrity". Although this scathing criticism was published, Dr Thompson was not invited to introduce the next edition.

In the annual Darwin Lecture, addressed to the British Association in September 1980, Dr John Durant of University College, Swansea, said to the assembled scientists: "Darwin's evolutionary explanation of the origin of man has been transformed into a modern myth, to the detriment of science and social progress".[11] Yet Dr Durant remains an evolutionist himself. The noted anthropologist Loren Eiseley wrote: "After having chided the theologian for his reliance on myth and miracle, science found itself in the unenviable position of having to create a mythology of its own: namely, the assumption that what, after long effort, could not be proved to take place today, had, in truth, taken place in the primaeval past".[12] The Swedish evolutionist Soren Lovtrup wrote: "I believe that one day the Darwinian myth will be ranked with the greatest deceit in the history of science".[13] But he remains an evolutionist, and this diatribe was but a preliminary to stating his own new theory of evolution.

Again and again evolutionists appear to take delight in debunking other theories before proposing their own version. An article entitled "Evolution as a religion" stated: "Evolution is the creation myth of our age. Science is based on faith, and evolution is a religion in itself".[14] It becomes clear that, while some scientists denounce Darwinism because they have a theory of their own to offer, others regard the theory of evolution in any form as scientific mythology. It is certainly not true, as often claimed, that all scientists believe in evolution.

### The evolution of the theory

Beginning as a Greek philosophy many centuries ago, the theory has passed through many stages, as *New Scientist* observed: "These

# SCIENCE AND EVOLUTION

**CHARLES** Darwin wrote: "*False facts are highly injurious to the progress of science, for they often long endure. But false views, if supported by some evidence, do little harm, as everyone takes a salutary pleasure in proving their falseness*" (cited in *Nature*, 24 November 1983, p. 314).

●

"*THE PAST 20 years or so have seen some spectacular examples of scientific fraud . . . The passionate desire to publicise a pet theory is one [factor]. Science still condones practices that are regarded simply as minor manipulations of data. This leniency, or bending of the rules, can slide into more serious abuse*" (*New Scientist*, 28 April 1990, p. 87). This tendency has been evident for over a century, or the theory of evolution would never have gained credence. However, the evolution fraud is being exposed bit by bit by, of all people, evolutionists who want to promulgate a new theory of their own, and have to point out the errors of previous theories.

●

**THE** reviewer of the book *Bully for Brontosaurus* by evolutionist S. J. Gould, says: "*Evolutionary language is so built into our Western vocabulary that we tend to assume we understand the concepts that the terms describe. We need books like this to remind us that sometimes we do not, and that there are con men playing with words in science as well as in politics*" (*New Scientist*, 22 June 1991, p. 47). Well said! Today's new theory becomes tomorrow's myth, and in the meantime there is a danger of being blinded by science.

●

"*THE secular myths of evolution have had a damaging effect on scientific research, leading to distortion, needless controversy and the gross misuse of science*" (Gerald Durant's Darwin Lecture to the British Association for the Advancement of Science, reported in *New Scientist*, 11 September 1980, p. 765).

are confusing times for those who take an interest in Darwinism
... such observers are faced with a bewildering variety of scientific
opinions, some Darwinian, some more or less Darwinian and some
quite unDarwinian".[15] Malcolm Muggeridge, famous philosopher
and broadcaster, in his Pascal Lecture at the University of Waterloo, Ontario, said: "I myself am convinced that the theory of
evolution . . . will be one of the great jokes in the history books of
the future ... Posterity will marvel that so very flimsy and dubious
an hypothesis could be accepted with the incredible credulity that
it has".

Yet new theories continue to be proposed, and discounted. The
possibility of an alternative explanation of the multiplicity of life on
earth is seldom considered. The only consistency about the views
of evolutionists is that somehow, somewhere and sometime evolution must have taken place—this in spite of the complete lack of
evidence to support the theory, and the mass of evidence against
it having taken place. The reason for this very unscientific attitude
was explained long ago by surgeon Sir Arthur Keith in these words:
"Evolution is unproved and unprovable, but we believe it because
the only alternative, special creation, is unthinkable".[16] A similar
view was expressed in *New Scientist*: "Evolutionists may disagree
on many things, but their commitment to atheism ensures their
solid agreement on the non-existence of an intelligent creator".[17]

"We simply believe that there was no relatively recent creation,
but cannot prove it. If not, then science would also appear to be a
religion", wrote Bruce Denness, of the Bureau of Applied Science.[18]
Perhaps he should have said science, meaning evolution, is a faith,
for the meaning of religion is a 'binding back' to God, from whom
man has broken loose. "Exciting as the scientific endeavour doubtlessly is, its vision of the Universe is ultimately devoid of inner
meaning. It lies in pieces at our feet, and is, in essence, dead". This
confession appeared under the title "A Matter of Life and Death".[19]
How true this depressing statement is, for the evolutionist has no
knowledge of how life began, nor its purpose, nor its future!

A very frank explanation of the standpoint of an evolutionist
was written by Aldous Huxley in *Confessions of a Professional
Atheist*.[20] He confessed: "I had motives for not wanting the world
to have meaning, consequently assumed it had none, and was

without difficulty able to find satisfying reasons for this assumption — the philosophy of meaninglessness was essentially an instrument of liberation . . . from a certain political and economic system and from certain systems of morality. We objected to the morality because it interfered with our sexual freedom".

It becomes clear from these and other similar views that the theory of evolution is tied to the philosophical view that there is no Creator, and therefore no creation. It is a faith in a negative, without any positive outlook at all. It has been given an aura of respectability by claiming that it is scientific. As we have seen in this brief sketch, evolution is not scientific by any stretch of the imagination, nor is it the view of all scientists. The tree of evolution has no roots, and only bears the most bitter of fruits.

## References

1. Dr Karl Popper, *New Scientist* (2 Oct. 1986), p. 36.
2. W. Stansfield (1977), *The Science of Evolution*, Macmillan, p. 3.
3. C. D. Darlington, *Scientific American* (July 1964).
4. *New Scientist* (4 Aug. 1988), p. 53.
5. Isaac Newton (1704) *Opticks*, New York reprint, p. 402.
6. *Nature* (7 Dec. 1989), p. 678.
7. C. Darwin (1959), *Origin of Species*, Watts & Co., London, p. 127.
8. *Nature* (12 Mar. 1981), p. 82.
9. *Ibid.*, p. 78.
10. *Nature* (5 Jan. 1989), p. 25.
11. *New Scientist* (11 Sept. 1980), p. 765.
12. Loren Eiseley (1957), *The Immense Journey*, Random House, New York, p. 199.
13. Soren Lovtrup (1988), *Darwinism, The Refutation of a Myth*, cited in *New Scientist* (15 Oct. 1988), p. 66.
14. *New Scientist* (13 Feb. 1986), p. 5.
15. 12 Sept. 1985, p. 59.
16. Sir Arthur Keith (1948), *A New Theory of Human Evolution*.
17. *New Scientist* (15 Mar. 1987), p. 63.
18. *Nature* (15 Dec. 1988), p. 614.
19. *New Scientist* (19 Apr. 1989), p. 62.
20. Aldous Huxley (1906), *Confessions of a Professional Atheist*, Watts & Co., London.

# 2

# EVOLUTION AND FOSSILS

It is often claimed that "fossils prove evolution"—a claim that is difficult to dispute unless one is well informed. It is in fact an appeal to ignorance, as Charles Darwin could see, for he wrote: "As by this theory innumerable transitional forms must have existed, why do we not find them embedded in countless numbers in the crust of the earth? The number of intermediate links between all living and extinct species must have been inconceivably great".[1] Darwin's theory of gradual evolution required countless fossil links between the species, and he knew that these links were missing, but hoped that further exploration would reveal them. But evolutionist writers tended to ignore Darwin's caution. For example, R. Manwell stated: "Fossils constitute the best evidence of evolution";[2] while D. D. Davies wrote: "The truth of evolution was proved conclusively by palaeontology".[3] School text books make similar statements, and so the fiction that fossils prove evolution has come to be accepted without question.

What do evolutionist writers now say about this claim? The noted evolutionist Stephen J. Gould wrote: ". . . the evolutionary trees that adorn our text books . . . are based on inference, however reasonable, not the evidence of fossils".[4] More recently, Mark Ridley said: "No real evolutionist, whether gradualist or punctuationist, uses the fossil record as evidence in favour of the theory of evolution as opposed to special creation".[5] This lack of evidence from fossils has been highlighted frequently by many scientists working in various fields of study. The lack of evidence that Darwin deplored is still lacking over a century later.

# EVOLUTION AND FOSSILS

## Scientists and the missing links

The following quotations are all taken from books written by writers who have the evolutionary point of view. To begin with, Darwin wrote: "Pray do not think that I am so blind as not to see that there are numerous immense difficulties in my notions".[6] He had written in his *Origin of Species*: "The distinctness of specific forms, and their not being blended together by innumerable transitional links, is a very obvious difficulty... Why then is not every geological formation and every stratum full of such intermediate links? Geology assuredly does not reveal any such finely graduated organic chain, and this, perhaps, is the most obvious and serious objection which can be urged against my theory".[7]

The following are quotations from specialists in various aspects of nature:

"Evolution requires intermediate forms between species, and palaeontology does not provide them".[8]

"The geological record has so far provided no evidence as to the origin of fishes".[9]

"There are no fossils known that show what the primitive ancestral insects looked like".[10]

"From the fossil record there is no direct proof of the origin of reptiles".[11]

"The fact is, there is no fossil evidence for the evolution of vertebrates, they all appear suddenly and fully specialised".[12]

"There is no missing link [connecting] mammals and reptiles".[13]

"There is no fossil evidence of the stages through which the remarkable change from reptile to bird was achieved".[14]

"The fossil ancestry of the first primitive mammals is completely unknown".[15]

From this selection of statements by a wide range of evolutionist writers it will be seen that Darwin's doubts about the evidence of fossils for his theory were justified. The fossils do not provide the essential evidence for evolution that he hoped for.

In the teaching of evolution to children and students a frequently used example that appeals to them is that of the horse. Text books claim that horses evolved from a little creature called *Eohippus*. Yet

**IN A** report on lectures at Darwin College, Cambridge, the reviewer says: "*Pilbeam presents the available evidence on the descent of humans, and in so doing makes it clear that we need a lot more of the same before we are on solid ground*" (*New Scientist*, 7 January 1989, p. 58). So the exponents of the theory admit that it is not on solid ground! Did the reviewer really intend to say "*descent of humans*"? Did not Darwin write about *The Ascent of Man*?

●

"***TWO*** *reports of new fossil evidence suggest that many, if not all of the so-called archaic primates . . . are not primates at all . . .*" (*Nature*, 24 May 1990, p. 340). One by one the supposed fossil ancestors of man are being phased out, but the school text books are not revised accordingly. Why not?

●

"***IN FACT*** *you might say that early primate evolution has just glided out of the window . . . A very small number of new specimens have so revised our views of what was thought to be a well understood time period . . .*" (*New Scientist*, 23 June 1990, p. 57). Perhaps the greatest surprise will be to discover that primate evolution never took place at all. May that day soon come!

●

"***IT REMAINS*** *true . . . that most new species, genera and families . . . appear in the record suddenly, and are not led up to by known gradual, completely continuous transitional sequences*" (G. G. Simpson, *The Major Features of Evolution*, 1953, p. 360).

●

"***NEW*** *species almost always appeared suddenly in the fossil record with no intermediate links to ancestors in older rocks of the same region*" (S. J. Gould, "Evolution's Erratic Pace", *Natural History Magazine*, May 1977, p. 12).

# EVOLUTION AND FOSSILS

for the past half-century this fraud has been exposed by many evolutionist writers such as M. Deperet: "The supposed evolution of the Equidae is a deceitful delusion".[16] (The Equidae are the family of horses, asses and zebras.) David M. Raup wrote: "Some of the classic cases of Darwinian change in the fossil record, such as the evolution of the horse, have had to be discarded".[17] The well-known evolutionist writer G. G. Simpson wrote: "The evolution of the horse family, Equidae, is now no better known than that of numerous other groups of organisms".[18]

It is the same story when we consider the apes, and man's supposed descent from them:

> "The fossil record which would enable us to trace the emergence of the apes is still hopelessly incomplete. We do not know when or where distinctively apelike animals first began to diverge from the monkey stock".[19]
>
> "The phylogenetic history of the New World monkeys, or Platyrhines, is quite unknown".[20]
>
> "As to the Old World monkeys, even less is known of their past".[21]
>
> "Man is as far separated from his supposed simian relatives as bats and whales are from other animals".[22]

This uncertainty and lack of evidence that is so well known to biologists and zoologists has not been communicated to the public or even to students. It is not just one missing link that evades the evolutionist, but a whole chain of missing links right through nature. Fossils do not prove evolution.

A computer's view . . .

## Hopeful monsters

The evolutionists' answer to this problem has been to discredit Darwin's concept of gradual change, and propose evolution by great jumps, or 'macroevolution'. In the 1930s Richard B. Goldschmidt challenged Darwinism and pointed out that an evolving eye, which was not yet able to see, would be a distinct disadvantage. So he offered his theory of tremendous mutations, whereby a blind creature received instant sight and a deaf creature received instant hearing. This was known as the 'Hopeful Monster' theory, and it lay dormant for years. Then it was revived by S. J. Gould and Miles Eldredge under the new name of 'Punctuated Equilibrium'. Even though there was no evidence to support this theory, it was offered as a sop to appease those evolutionists who were still concerned about the lack of links. The new theory did not require links, which were replaced by sudden jumps.

Darwin had evidently considered such a theory and pronounced it impossible when he wrote his *Origin of Species*. His view was expressed in Latin: *Natura non facit saltum* (Nature does not make jumps). But that is not the end of the story, for S. J. Gould could see flaws in his new theory and tried to sort these out in a revision of his book entitled *Macroevolution Dynamism*. His co-author of the earlier theory, Miles Eldredge, did not cooperate on this one and was quite critical of it.

Under whatever banner, the idea of a monkey giving birth to a human, or a reptile laying an egg that hatched out as a bird, is rather far fetched, to put it mildly, and that is what these theories would have implied. So it must be realised that fossils are not really very helpful to the evolutionist.

What do the fossils reveal to us?

1. that many forms of life are now extinct;
2. that the extinctions were exceedingly rapid, and due to circumstances that are not now prevalent;
3. that fossils are not evidence of evolution.

"At the present stage of geological research, we have to admit that there is nothing in the geological records that runs contrary to the view of conservative creationists, that God created each species separately, presumably from the dust of the earth".[23]

# EVOLUTION AND FOSSILS

**References**
1. C. Darwin (1859), *Origin of Species*, Watts & Co., London, p. 127.
2. R. Manwell, *Introduction to Protozoology*, p. 36.
3. D. D. Davies (1949), *Genetics, Palaeontology and Evolution*, Princeton University Press, p. 87.
4. *National Geographic Magazine* (May 1977), p. 13.
5. *New Scientist* (25 June 1981), p. 831.
6. C. Darwin (1882), *Life and Letters*, Vol. 2, p. 34.
7. C. Darwin (1859), *Origin of Species*, Watts & Co., London, p. 251.
8. D. B. Kitts, *Evolution 28*, p. 467.
9. J. R. Norman (1963) (British Museum Zoologist), *A History of Fishes*, p. 296.
10. Life Nature Library, *The Insects*, p. 14.
11. R. A. Sturton, *Time, Life and Man*, Wiley, New York, p. 416.
12. Professor A. H. Cook, *Cambridge Natural History*, Vol. 3, p. 5.
13. Life Nature Library, *The Reptiles*, p. 47.
14. W. E. Swinton (1960), *Biology and Comparative Physiology*, Vol. 1, Academic Press, p. 1.
15. H. Stubbings (1971), *Organic Evolution*, p. 145.
16. M. Deperet (1980), *Transformations in the Animal World*, Arno, New York, p. 105.
17. *The Field Museum of Natural History Bulletin* (Jan. 1979).
18. G. G. Simpson (1953), *Life of the Past*, Yale University Press, p. 127.
19. Life Nature Library, *The Primates*, p. 15.
20. W. L. Strauss, *Anthropology Today*, p. 77.
21. W. Howells (1954), *Mankind in the Making*, p. 102.
22. Professor Vialleton, *Membres et Leintures des Vertebres Tetrapodes*, Libraire octave Doin, Paris, p. 281.
23. Edmund Ambrose (1982), *The Nature and Origin of the Biological World*, Wiley, New York, p. 64.

# 3

# DO MUTATIONS AND NATURAL SELECTION PRODUCE EVOLUTION?

There is a widely held view that evolution is easily explained as the cumulative result of many successive minor variations building up to a major variation, with an eventual change from one species to another. Expressed in more scientific terms, it is said that many micromutations make a macromutation.

*The Oxford Dictionary of Natural History* states categorically that "Mutations are the raw material for evolution. They provide the source of all variations. For mutations to affect subsequent generations, though, they must occur in gametes [sex cells], or in cells destined to be gametes, since only then will they be inherited . . . Most mutations are deleterious, evolution progresses through the few that are favourable". Then it explains what causes mutations: "A mutagen is an agent that increases the mutation rate within an organism. Examples of mutagens are X-rays, gamma rays, neutrons and certain chemicals such as carcinogens".[1]

### Do mutations produce evolution?

In school, college and university, students are taught that evolution could have taken place slowly over millions of years by a series of small mutations until one species has changed into another species. Professor Dobzhansky stated: "Mutation produces changes in the genes and variants in the gene structure, these are the raw material of evolution".[2] It is true that mutations do take place, but mutations in the ordinary living cells of the body, such as those causing cancer,

# MUTATIONS AND NATURAL SELECTION

are not passed on to the next generation. Mutations in the sex cells can be inherited, but they are more often than not harmful. To quote again from Professor Dobzhansky: "Mutational changes in any one gene are rare events. This is a different way of saying that ordinarily the genes reproduce themselves accurately".[3]

Of a conference of top-level scientists at Chicago in 1980 it was reported that "The central question . . . was whether the mechanisms of microevolution [mutations and natural selection] could be extrapolated to explain the phenomena of macroevolution. At the risk of doing violence to the positions of some people at the meeting, the answer can be given of a clear NO".[4] Arthur Koestler has written: "The educated public continues to believe that Darwin has provided all the relevant answers by the magic formula of random mutations plus natural selection, quite unaware of the fact that random mutations turned out to be irrelevant, and natural selection a tautology".[5] Professor P. P. Grasse, who held the Chair of Evolution at Paris, stated simply: "No matter how numerous they may be, mutations do not produce any kind of evolution".[6]

Fruit flies. The mutation on the right has vestigial wings and would therefore be unable to fly.

Nevertheless, Dr H. J. Muller decided to put the theory to a test, and for about fifty years he subjected fruit flies to irradiation by X-rays in order deliberately to produce mutations in the hope of producing evolution. He succeeded in producing millions of mutations, but the fruit flies stubbornly refused to evolve. Those that survived the ordeal were nothing more nor less than badly deformed fruit flies. Of the millions of mutations, Dr Muller could only claim that two were viable. These survived under laboratory conditions, but were unfit for survival in the wild.

Dr Muller's report said: "In more that 99% of the cases the mutation of a gene produces some kind of harmful effect, some disturbance of function".[7] For his lifetime of work trying to prove evolution by mutation he was given the Nobel Prize, and summarised his findings thus: "Most mutations are bad. In fact, good ones

"*IT IS* good to keep in mind . . . that nobody has ever succeeded in producing even one new species by the accumulation of micromutations. Darwin's theory of natural selection has never had any proof, yet it has been universally accepted" (Professor R. Goldschmidt in *Material Basis of Evolution*, Yale University Press, p. 211).

•

"*EVOLUTIONARY* biologists have found it hard to wrestle with the theory of 'punctuated equilibrium' (advanced by Eldredge a few years ago) for like Proteus, it changes form when firmly grasped . . . Punctuated equilibrium's newest incarnation, described as 'Macroevolutionary Dynamics' is missing further parts . . . The new truncated theory is barely recognisable as punctuated equilibrium" (review of Mike Eldredge's book *Macroevolutionary Dynamics* in *Nature*, 20 April 1989, p. 672). How strange that the inventor of the new theory that made mincemeat of all previous theories of evolution now makes mincemeat of his own theory!

•

"*FOR* well over 100 years, many biologists have been genuinely unhappy with evolution by natural selection, or Darwinism. They feel it is far too simplistic to say that the grandeur of evolution can be explained by a somewhat haphazard genetic variation followed by selective reproduction success. The same problem arises with the magic of an egg turning into a tree or a giraffe. How is it possible that genes can give off the kind of information needed for these wonderful developmental transformations?" (review of the book *Dynamic Structures in Biology* in *Nature*, 7 December 1989, p. 628). That is a good question! Genes cannot give off information that has not been programmed into them, and this precludes the possibility of an accidental evolution. The very fact that the genes have information proves that they were provided with that information by an intelligence, and that points unmistakably to the Creator.

# MUTATIONS AND NATURAL SELECTION

are so rare that we can consider them all bad".[8] Another writer has said: "If by evolution we mean macroevolution, then it can be said with the utmost rigour that the doctrine is totally without scientific sanction. Now, to be sure, given the multitude of extravagant claims about evolution promulgated by evolutionists with an air of scientific infallibility, this may indeed sound strange. And yet the fact remains that there exists to this day not a shred of scientific evidence in support of the thesis that macroevolutionary transformations have ever occurred".[9]

In the words and work of eminent evolutionists the claim that the process of evolution has taken place by numerous mutations can be seen for what it is worth. Mutations cause devolution, but not evolution.

## Is natural selection a factor in evolution?

The well-known evolutionist Stephen J. Gould of Harvard University wrote: "The essence of Darwinism lies in a single phrase, 'Natural Selection is the creative force of evolutionary change'. Of course nobody denies that natural selection will play a role in eliminating the unfit. But Darwinian theories require that it creates the fit as well".[10] Dr Colin Patterson of the British Museum of Natural History said in a television interview on 4 March 1982: "No one has ever produced a species by mechanisms of natural selection. No one has ever gotten near it, and most of the current argument in Neo-Darwinism is about this question". Then Dr Patterson wrote in a personal letter: "It is easy enough to make up stories of how one form gave rise to another, and to find reason why the stages should be favoured by natural selection. But such stories are not part of science, for there is no way of putting them to the test".

As a living example of natural selection in action, students are told of the case of the Peppered Moth in industrial Britain as a proof of evolution. J. Harrison Matthews wrote: "The Peppered Moth experiments beautifully demonstrate natural selection, or survival of the fittest, but they do not show evolution in progress. For, however the population may alter in their content of light, intermediate or dark forms, all the moths remain, from beginning to end, *Biston betularia*".[11]

96    IS EVOLUTION A SCIENCE?

Two forms of the Peppered Moth. The darker form became much more abundant in the polluted atmosphere of industrialised cities.

**Summary**

"Species do indeed have a capacity to undergo minor modifications in their physical and other characteristics, but this is limited, and with a longer perspective it is reflected as an oscillation about a mean".[12] That there is considerable flexibility within each species is evident from a casual look at the variation among dogs. However, they all remain dogs, and recognise one another as such. The eminent evolutionist Richard Goldschmidt admitted that "the facts fail to give any information regarding the origin of actual species... or higher categories",[13] and J. Wolfgang Smith said: "The fact remains that there exists to this day not a shred of scientific evidence in support of the thesis that macroevolutionary transformations have ever occurred".[9]

The scientific evidence from many evolutionists is sufficient to show that occasional mutations and ongoing natural selection do not amount to any evolution from one species into another. However, these factors do serve to eliminate the unhealthy features in a species, although sometimes they have been used to man's advantage. Examples include seedless grapes, pipless oranges, and hornless cattle and sheep. Such mutations, however, are a disadvantage to the plant or animal, and would soon be eliminated if left

# MUTATIONS AND NATURAL SELECTION

to nature. Mutations such as these are not evidence of evolution, any more than those poor deformed fruit flies in Dr Muller's fifty-year experiment to try to make them evolve; and the phrase 'survival of the fittest' is tautology because in this phrase the word 'fittest' means 'fittest to survive'.

## References

1. *Oxford Dictionary of Natural History*, p. 410.
2. Professor Dobzhansky (1957), *The Biological Basis of Human Freedom*, p. 56.
3. Wallace & Dobzhansky (1960), *Radiation, Genes and Man*, p. 35.
4. *Science* (21 Nov. 1980), pp. 883-7.
5. Arthur Koestler (1978), *Janus*, Vintage Books, New York, p. 185.
6. Professor P. P. Grasse (1977), *Evolution of Living Organisms*, Academic Press, New York, p. 162.
7. *Scientific American* (Nov. 1955), p. 58.
8. *Time* (11 Nov. 1946), p. 38.
9. J. Wolfgang Smith (1988), *Teilhardism and the New Religion*, Pan Books, p. 5.
10. *Natural History* (June/July 1971), p. 28.
11. J. Harrison Matthew (1971), *Introduction to Origin of Species*, Dent.
12. *Science* (21 Nov. 1980).
13. Richard Goldschmidt (1940), *The Material Basis of Evolution*, Yale Univeristy Press, p. 165.

# 4

# UNSOLVED PROBLEMS OF EVOLUTION

The theory of evolution is assumed by many to be a self-evident fact of nature. It is unusual for students of biology to hear of any other possible alternative. Evolution is credited with being the only rational scientific explanation of the many diverse forms of life on earth.

Most people accept the theory of evolution because they think that most people accept the theory of evolution. It is a subject seldom discussed because it is assumed that the theory has been proved by science, irrespective of the total lack of evidence in favour of it.

The two previous chapters have highlighted the problems of
1. the lack of evidence from fossils, in spite of wild claims;
2. the scientific rebuttal of mutations and natural selection as the mechanism of evolution.

In addition, chapter 2 of "Is Creation Credible?" showed that science has no explanation for the origin of life. It is now proposed to look at a number of further problems, which tend to be ignored by the advocates of evolution because of the evidence they provide to nullify the scientific nature of the theory.

Francis Bacon wrote: "It is true that a little philosophy inclineth men's mind to atheism, but depth in philosophy bringeth men's mind about to religion".[1] However, depth in philosophy need not take us out of our depth, as will be seen. The reasoning to be advanced is well within the understanding of a non-technical person. It consists of pointing out simple things that tend to be ignored by the "little philosophy" of the evolutionist, things that are too often "swept under the carpet", as very pointedly remarked by Sir Andrew Huxley.[2]

### Cause and effect

To quote the early evolutionist S. J. Mivart: "One of these self-evident necessary truths is that every change or new existence requires a cause".[3] For every effect there must be a cause. Moreover, the cause must be adequate to produce the effect. Here the Law of Conservation of Energy (the First Law of Thermodynamics) applies. Energy can neither be created nor destroyed in the system in which we live on earth. It has long been realised that matter is a form of energy, and is interchangeable with other forms of energy. The obvious consequence of this law is that the total energy in the universe remains the same as it was when it was originated, in one form or another.

What was the cause that produced this effect? There are two alternatives:

1. that the universe was brought into existence complete with its total energy, as at present;
2. that the universe has always existed as it is now.

The second alternative is shown to be scientifically false by the Law of Entropy (the Second Law of Thermodynamics), which is to be seen everywhere in the deterioration of all forms of energy—not destroyed, but no longer available. For example, all forms of life eventually die, machines wear out, buildings deteriorate and fall down, heat is dissipated, iron rusts. The energy changes its form. The famous Harvard University physicist P. W. Bridgman wrote: "The two Laws of Thermodynamics are, I suppose, accepted by physicists as perhaps the most secure generalisations from experience that we have. The physicist does not hesitate to apply the two laws to any concrete physical situation in the confidence that nature will not let him down".[4]

So, according to science, the universe was brought into existence complete with its total energy, as at present. The source of the energy that holds the atomic structure of matter together is not fully understood, but it is known that "the attractive energy that holds any one particle together in the nucleus [of the atom] is, in general, of the order of 6 to 8 million volts".[5] The fact that all scientific investigation is only possible because the universe and nature is governed by laws cannot be explained by the supposition that chance, accidents of nature, or randomness, can account for the orderliness, the design and the information that is everywhere to be seen. Laws, designs, processes, systems and information require intelligence, indeed, a superintelligence, to produce them. The effect cannot be greater than the cause.

It follows that the First Cause cannot have been a chemical reaction or a mechanical explosion (by whatever name), but must have been an intelligent, conscious source of tremendous energy. Sheer logic points to a personal Creator, to a Creator Who is concerned for His creation, to a Creator Who has created for a purpose, and Who is almighty. It is man's familiarity with the countless natural laws with which he is surrounded that has led to a complacency which ignores the lawmaker. It is so easy to take everything for granted, because most of us have never known anything different. But this is very shallow thinking. The evidence is everywhere around us that an adequate cause for all we can perceive is required.

Sir James Jeans, the eminent astronomer, wrote: "Today, there is a wide measure of agreement, which on the physical side of science approaches almost to unanimity, that the stream of knowledge is heading towards a non-mechanical reality; the Universe begins to look more like a great thought than like a great machine".[6]

### Information

Dr Paul Davies of King's College, London asked: "Where did all the information that makes the world such a special place come from originally?".[7] All forms of life on earth are crammed full of information. While this may not be obvious to the casual observer, science has revealed that nature is totally based on information. For example, a tiny grass seed contains within itself complex information on how to grow, how to send leaves upwards and roots downwards, how to synthesise food from light, air and water, how

## Maize

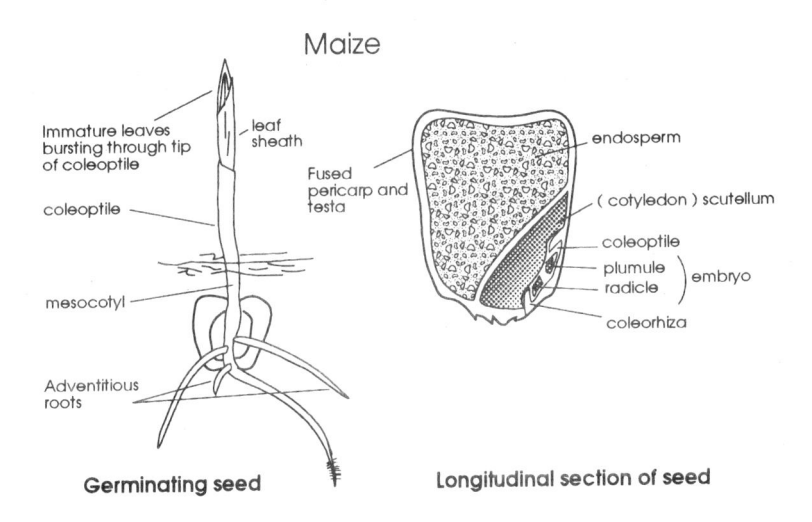

**Germinating seed** (labels): Immature leaves bursting through tip of coleoptile; leaf sheath; coleoptile; mesocotyl; Adventitious roots

**Longitudinal section of seed** (labels): endosperm; (cotyledon) scutellum; coleoptile; plumule; radicle; embryo; coleorhiza; Fused pericarp and testa

to produce flowers and seeds, each of which has to be packed with a replica of the same complex information.

Living cells are active in some very complicated ways. Even the so-called 'primitive' forms of life, such as green algae, are not 'simple' in the way they behave and replicate, all of which requires that the living cells have the information within themselves. The cell needs complex information for the manufacture of proteins. "When a cell needs to make a particular protein, something else has to 'read' the relevant genes and translate each codon. Then the appropriate amino acid must be found, and all the amino acids must be assembled together in the correct order to make the protein".[8] "For an organism to grow, repair damaged tissues and reproduce, its cells must proliferate. Division begins with the process of mitosis, in which the previously duplicated chromosomes are separated from each other and parcelled into two matching, well-segregated packages. Just how this spindle-shaped biological machine parcels the DNA of a dividing cell into two equal clusters is only now becoming clear. The spindle turns out to be as dynamic as it is accurate".[9]

The sheer mass of information contained in the DNA molecule is mind-boggling. "The genome comprises 3,500 million molecular groups known as 'bases' or nucleotides . . . when arranged in sequences of tens of thousands of bases, these nucleotides represent genes. These genes are arranged as chromosomes, of which each individual [human] has 46, arranged in pairs".[10] It has been claimed that, if the information contained in the human DNA was to be printed in small print in a human instruction manual for the growth and development of the cells of the body, it would require 500 books, each of 1,000 pages, to spell out the detailed information. When it is realised that all this information is packed into the one DNA molecule within each cell of the body, we should join with the psalmist and exclaim: "I will praise Thee; for I am fearfully and wonderfully made: marvellous are Thy works; and that my soul knoweth right well" (Ps. 139:14).[11]

### Proteins and nucleotides

Science has found that two of the basic materials of life are proteins and nucleotides. Protein is required before nucleotides can be formed, and nucleotides are necessary for the formation of protein. Both of these very complex materials must have been present from the very beginning of life. As it is inconceivable that both of these intricate chemical substances should have come into existence accidentally at the very same time, a beginning of life by chance is scientifically impossible. The first living cell was dependent upon both of these vital substances being available at precisely the same

> **WITHIN** a cell, the nucleic acids code for the making of the enzymes, and the enzymes manufacture the nucleic acids, all with incredible speed and precision. The first cell must have required not only the nucleic acids but also the different enzymes which work in concert to make the DNA. "*There is a hitch*", reports *Scientific American* in an article in February 1991, which surveys a number of recent theories of how life began. "*Proteins cannot form without DNA, but neither can DNA form without proteins. To those pondering the origin of life, it is a classic chicken-and-egg problem. Which came first, proteins or DNA?*". On a number of counts it is clear that the primeval-soup theory, proposed in the name of science, is no more scientific than the pre-Pasteur ideas of the spontaneous generation of lice in old socks.

# UNSOLVED PROBLEMS OF EVOLUTION 103

moment in time. Thus the deeper scientific investigation goes into the mysteries of life the more impossible the theory of evolution becomes.

Countless experiments have been made by scientists who are trying to prove that a living cell could have been formed 'in a warm pond' by a chance aggregation of a number of amino acids. While some of the results have been the formation of interesting materials, not one of them has produced even a dead cell, and certainly not a living cell.

It can be pointed out that all the ingredients for the so-called pre-biotic soup, from which life is supposed to have merged, can be found in a tin of meat soup. The problem is merely that of bringing it to life. It is over a century ago that the French scientist Louis Pasteur proved that life cannot spring from non-life. His comment at the time was simply: "Never will the doctrine of spontaneous generation arise from this mortal blow". "There was no primeval soup, neither on this planet nor on any other, and if the beginnings of life were not random, they must therefore have been the product of purposeful intelligence", wrote Fred Hoyle.[12]

### Consciousness and thought

If it is true that life evolved originally from non-living elements of the earth, the question must arise, Where did the ability to think come from? The origin of consciousness, or imagination, of ability to reason, and even of the instinct in animals, cannot be explained by the theory of evolution. Even a honey bee, with its brain the size of a pinhead, can navigate, and can communicate with and be understood by its hivemates. How did such immaterial abilities develop from material origins, as supposed by evolutionists? This vital problem has never been seriously addressed by evolutionists, and is one of the many outstanding problems that have been conveniently "swept under the carpet" by scientists.

The only rational and logical conclusion that can account for the origin of the ability to think is that life originated from a superintelligent First Cause, who was able to implant these abilities. Indeed, logic points to a personal all-powerful Creator, Who had the ability to think, to reason, to communicate, as well as to design and to create. It is evident that there is no way in which inanimate chemicals could organise themselves into a brain, when the complexity of the nerve circuits of the brain is appreciated. The number of possible nerve connections in a human brain is so vast that it would require several pages of this book to carry the number of zeros involved.

Japanese scientists are trying to construct a computer with the abilities of a brain. They are not modelling it on a human brain, but on the brain of a nematode, a tiny, threadlike creature about one millimetre long, which has a brain occupying one third of its length. Its brain instructs the nematode to wriggle away from hostile environments, to seek out nutrition and to reproduce itself. "No manufactured computer can handle anything like this complexity of information", reported *New Scientist*.[13]

Inside your micro . . .

Every form of life has its own complexity of information within itself, instructing it how to grow, how to feed, in some cases how to fend off enemies, and how to reproduce. Even more than that, each form of life can impart to its progeny the same complexity of information. That is some of the wonder of life, which is quite inexplicable by the theory of a mechanical, or chemical, origin.

### Biometry

The study of biology from a statistical point of view, known as biometry, has demonstrated the practical impossibility of many of the assumptions that are taken for granted by evolutionists. Professor Morowitz estimated the statistical possibility of the accidental formation of a simple cell.[14] His figure was one chance in a number that ended with 340 million zeros, likened to tossing a coin a billion times and getting heads every time. It is manifest that such a result

"... **HUMAN** beings have only a very poor knowledge of how their own brains work. There are many mechanisms in our heads that are essential for thinking (and for consciousness and speech), but we don't yet know what they are. If it is the case that the brain is more complicated than we believe it to be, then the task for evolutionists becomes even harder, because some of the mechanisms that they ought ideally to be explaining, have not yet been properly described" (New Scientist, 15 April 1989, p. 58).

•

"**LIEBERMAN'S** ideas on the representation, learning and breakdown of language in modern man, which are influenced by his evolutionary and comparative studies, are also provocative . . . forcefully reminding those of his colleagues, who may have forgotten, there is a biological basis for what makes us human" (from a review of a book entitled Uniquely Human: The Evolution of Speech, Thought and Selfless Behaviour, in Nature, 11 April 1991, p. 535). Thought and communication are not found in inanimate matter, and evolution has no theory as to how humans became endowed with these faculties.

•

"**MOST** simply, the tautology is the observation that if in the 'survival of the fittest', the fittest are identified with the survivors, the principle of natural selection amounts to the empty slogan 'survival of the survivors'. This proposition does not explain why there should be survivors" (Nature, 25 April 1991, p. 653). The Second Law of Thermodynamics states the scientific fact that all things deteriorate, which in practice is devolution rather than evolution. That the survivors are the fittest is not true, except in the case of deliberate selection by breeders.

could not be accidental, but evidence of purposeful design in the formation of the living cell by a Creator.

**Common ancestry**

"The theory that all humans are descended from a recent African ancestor was promoted by geneticists who study living populations. The fossil record provides independent support for this model".[15] "Mitochondrial DNA, like Jewishness, is inherited down the female line. As we each have one mother, two grandmothers and so on, then we must all share a remote female ancestor in common ... it does seem that for most genes ... the ancestral populations are in Africa (or possibly in the Middle East)".[16]

Thus scientists are inevitably, although perhaps reluctantly, coming to the realisation that humans are of common stock, and originated in the area that the Bible describes geographically as the garden in Eden.

**Hybridism**

"Hybridism ... is one of the greatest obstacles to the general acceptance and progress of the great principle of evolution", wrote Charles Darwin.[17] Why should Darwin make this observation? A hybrid is the offspring of parents of different species or genera. Hybrids, such as the mule (a cross between a jackass and a mare) or hinny (a stallion and a female ass), are normally sterile. Occasionally such hybrids have been fertile, in which case the offspring have reverted to the species of one of the parents of the hybrid.

Naturally occurring hybrids are to be found between varieties of the same species, such as ducks in the animal world, and blackberries and oaks in the plant world. But their progeny do not always breed to the hybrid type. Many cultivated plants are hybrids (bananas, peanuts, dahlias and roses, for example), but these are not propagated by seeds, only by cuttings and root division, as the seeds do not produce the hybrid form. Seeds produced from artificially cross-pollinated plants are known as F1 seeds, and packets of these bear a printed warning that seeds taken from the plants so produced may not conform to the hybrid variety, but may revert, in accordance with Mendel's law of inheritance.

# UNSOLVED PROBLEMS OF EVOLUTION

No wonder that Charles Darwin was disconcerted by his consideration of hybridism, for it is evidence of natural devolution rather than evolution. Nevertheless, in spite of the evidence, evolutionists still sometimes claim that hybridism is the cause of evolution of new species, and many students are not sufficiently well informed to rebut the claim.

## References

1. Francis Bacon (1597), *Essays I*, p. 273.
2. Sir Andrew Huxley (3 Dec. 1981), *Nature*, p. 395.
3. S. J. Mivart (1882), *Nature and Thought*, p. 180.
4. *American Scientist* (Oct. 1953), "Reflections on Thermodynamics", p. 549.
5. R. E. Peierles, *The Laws of Nature*, Scribner, New York, p. 240.
6. Sir James Jeans (1932), *The Mysterious Universe*, Cambridge University Press, p. 140.
7. *New Scientist* (16 Nov. 1978), p. 506.
8. *New Scientist* (3 Dec. 1988), "How Cells Make Protein", p. 2.
9. *Scientific American* (Oct. 1989), "The Mitotic Spindle", p. 26.
10. *New Scientist* (4 Aug. 1990), p. 37.
11. For more details on the cell and DNA see *Is Creation Credible?*, Chapter 6.
12. *Nature* (12 Nov. 1981), p. 148.
13. *New Scientist*, (26 Jan. 1991), p. 51.
14. Professor Morowitz (1968), *Energy Flow in Biology*, Academic Press, New York, p. 990.
15. *Scientific American* (Dec. 1990), p. 76.
16. *Nature* (31 May 1990), p. 395.
17. C. Darwin (1877), *Cross- and Self-Fertilisation*, p. 27.

# 5

# THE TIME FACTOR

"The Age of the Earth Debate" was a leading article in *Scientific American* in which it was stated: "The controversy has aged the Earth 4.5 billion years during the past three centuries".[1] The reason for this ageing of the earth was made clear in an article in *Nature* entitled "Radio-dating the Galaxy". It explained that the theory of evolution required a very long time for the process to take place, but admitted that "the currently accepted physics of stellar evolution [is] incomplete, but the Universe may be substantially younger than presently believed".[2]

"Age of Universe Crisis Worsens" was the heading for an article in *New Scientist* which stated: "The two major astronomical approaches to estimating the age of the Universe disagree by 3,000 million years".[3] Presumably both of these approaches to the subject were strictly scientific; so which should one believe?

The issue is clear. The theory of evolution requires an infinity of time for the long-drawn-out process to take place. Evolutionists claim that, given enough time, anything could happen. By contrast, the record of creation is historical, and is supported by science in a number of ways that are seldom considered.

One might reasonably expect to receive many proofs of these long ages of billions of years from scientific evidence. It might be thought that the modern way of dating rocks by the radioisotopes would be proof. However, the concept of long ages was postulated long before this method of dating rocks was invented. It might be thought that the age of rocks can be judged by their appearance, or

# THE TIME FACTOR

by their place in the geologic column, or by the mineral content, but this is not so.

Since 1911 evolutionists have attempted to lend credibility to their assumed long ages by radiometric dating. This method is itself based on evolutionary assumptions, and the science magazines have from time to time cast doubts on the results. An article entitled "Dating Sediments by the K Ar Method" fully exposed the unsatisfactory nature of this method of dating rocks.[4] Then, in an article on radiometric dating, it was stated: "Radiometric dates are shown to be consistent with a considerably younger age for the Precambrian boundary than previously accepted".[5]

## The dating of rocks

So, if radiometric dating is not satisfactory, how are rocks dated? They are dated by the Index Fossil System, an idea formulated by a canal surveyor, William Smith (1769-1839). By this system, certain creatures are supposed to have been in existence so many million years ago, therefore the rocks containing their fossils can be dated to that time. "Whenever a rock is found bearing such a fossil, its approximate age is automatically established".[6] That sounds like an easy way to solve the problem of age, but:

"The intelligent layman has long suspected circular reasoning in the use of rocks to date fossils, and fossils to date rocks. The geologist has never bothered to think of a good reply";[7]

"Geologists are here arguing in a circle. The succession of organisms has been determined by the study of their remains in the rocks, and the relative ages of the rocks are determined by the remains of organisms they contain";[8]

"Palaeontologists (and evolutionary biologists in general) are famous for their facility in devising plausible stories, but they often forget that plausible stories need not be true".[9]

The weakness of this system came to light with the discovery that the fossil fish, the Coelacanth, supposedly extinct seventy million years ago, has been found alive and well in the deep ocean waters around the island of Madagascar. For years it had been regarded as an Index Fossil, and the rocks in which its fossils were found were dated to the supposed date of its extinction. There are quite

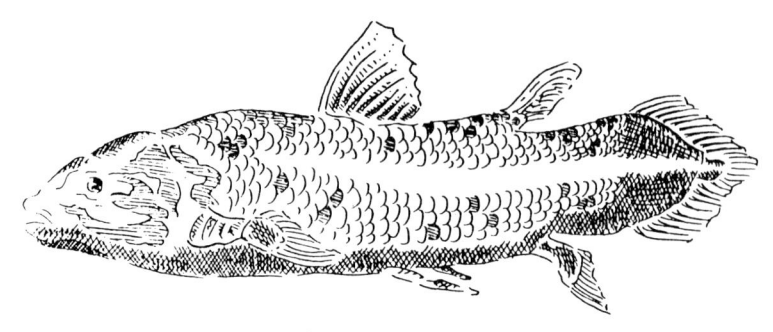

The Coelacanth.

a lot of other creatures that at one time were only known as fossils, but have now been discovered to be still around. Thus the Index Fossil System is not really scientific, since the supposed time of extinction is unknown, but is only surmised on the basis of the very questionable theory of evolution. Dating the rocks by their fossils, and the fossils by the rocks in which they are found, is not good science. It is an attempt to prove evolution by assuming that evolution has taken place.

### Why are fossils found in rocks?

The remains of plants and animals do not normally become fossils when buried. Fossils are only formed when abnormally large sediments envelop them rapidly under great pressure. Thus fossils have only been formed under exceptional circumstances, with ample evidence that the sediments in which they were trapped were water-borne. "Fossil Aches and Pains" was the title of an article with a photo of an adult Ichthyosaur in process of giving birth at the very moment of sudden death. Mother and offspring were fossilised together, evidence of a very sudden catastrophic burial.[10]

The worldwide evidence of fossils is that a catastrophe of great magnitude occurred, bringing sudden death to all manner of life, both plants and animals, burying all in sediments, to be compressed by further sediments. The speed with which the disaster occurred is demonstrated by the beautifully preserved fossils of spiders and even spiders' webs.[11] The discovery of the fossils of sea creatures on high hills is good evidence of the extent of the catastrophe that buried them; and the extensive fossil graveyards of countless creatures of differing species all huddled together belies the theory that fossils were formed by a normal process of burial.

### Polystrate fossils

The fossils of whole fully grown trees have been found. Some of these are prone, like those on the shoreline of Mull (near Dervaig). But, amazingly, there are some fossil trees that are upright; and, not only so, but they pierce several strata of rock. An example can be found on the island of Mull, in the cliff face at Ardmeanach. This would seem to be clear evidence that the strata of rock were laid rapidly in succession without displacing the tree. It is inconceivable that millions of years were involved in the fossilisation of the tree.

Other similar examples can be found in Yellowstone National Park and in Alabama (U.S.A.). But perhaps the most amazing example is that which was reported in *Chemical and Engineering News*, headed, "Workers Find Whale in Diatomaceous Earth Quarry".[12] In this deep quarry, as the diatomite was being mined, the complete fossil of a whale, about eighty feet long, was found standing on its tail. Diatomite is composed of millions of tiny diatom shells, and for the whale to be fossilised complete it must have been deposited and covered very rapidly. No normal process of gradual deposition of diatoms could account for this, for the whale would have decomposed if not covered and sealed very quickly. This fact conveys a picture of a tremendous watery catastrophe. No other explanation is viable.

### Dating of new rocks

Of particular interest in the dating of rocks are some observations of rock formations that have been formed within historic times. For example, the brand new volcanic island of Surtsey in the ocean south of Iceland was only formed in 1963. It has been under close observation ever since it was formed. Geologists and naturalists have been amazed to find that it already has the appearance of great age. "A whole island had been created and an extensive area of land had been formed from the primary rock. From the depths of the ocean there had been built up a broad base, on the top of which was an island with mountains and craters, lava flows, cliffs, gentle slopes, flat sandy beaches and weathered coastal strips with worn rounded pebbles and boulder rims that gave the landscape an ancient appearance".[13] The Icelandic geologist Sigurdur Thorarinsson had written ten years previously: "Only a few months have sufficed for a landscape to be created which is so varied and mature that it is almost beyond belief".[14] The island of Surtsey is evidence that it does not take millions of years for rocks to look old.

New lava rock formed by a volcano in 1801 on Hawaii was dated to 160 million years old by one method, and to three billion years old by another method.[15] Many other anomalous dates have been recorded, such as the frozen peat in which a frozen mammoth was found, which was dated to 3,600 years, while the hair of the frozen mammoth was dated to 26,000 years.

In practice, radiometric dates are usually abandoned if they do not agree with the preconceived notions of what they ought to be, but accepted if they concur. The system cannot be used with confidence as there are so many unknown variable factors. A scientific check on the accuracy and reliability of radiometric dating was reported in an article in *New Scientist* entitled "Unexpected Errors Affect Dating Techniques" as follows: "The margin of error with radiocarbon dating may be two or three times as great as the practitioners of the technique have claimed . . . a trial compared the accuracy with which 38 labs around the world dated artifacts of known age. Of the 38, only 7 produced results considered to be satisfactory".[16] An article entitled "Dating Volcanic Ash by ESR" said: "A new method of attempting to date volcanic ash . . . should be accepted with caution because several important sources of error have not been discussed, or properly handled".[17] In conclusion, it has to be admitted that dates confidently offered to the public are not so strictly scientific as might appear.

### Coal and oil

It is commonly asserted that coal and oil are good evidence that many millions of years must have elapsed for their formation. But several recent scientific experiments have demonstrated that both

"**THE** main skeleton in the closet of cosmology is the age of the Universe. Something has to give soon and it will be fascinating to see whether it is the theorists or the observers who back down first" (*Nature*, 1 August 1991, p. 378). Maybe all materialistic scientists will have to back down when the Creator intervenes.

●

**HALLEY'S** Comet is quite young: "*The rate at which comets such as Halley's lose material near perihelion is so great that they cannot have been in their present orbits for long*" (*Nature*, 11 May 1989, p. 95).

●

"**HERE** we report the evaluation of hydrothermal oil which we find to be similar to conventionally exploited crude oils. Its young geological age (c. 5,000 years Carbon-14 dating) indicates that a significant fraction of the organic carbon in the oil has completed the transformation from biomass to migrating oil in less than 5,000 years" (*Nature*, 2 November 1989, p. 65; see also *Nature*, 30 November 1989, p. 529). While this might astound evolutionists, who regard the formation of oil and coal as taking millions of years, it would not astound those scientists who have actually turned biomass into oil in a matter of hours by the use of heat and pressure.

●

"**MEASUREMENTS** of the stars indicate that the Universe is twice as old as many astronomers thought. The new work is controversial, because observations of the same galaxy a few months ago suggest that the Universe is 'young'" (*New Scientist*, 18 July 1992, p. 16). The same evidence is seen as proving both 'old' and 'young'.

these substances can be formed in a short time if the requisite heat and pressure are applied. Laboratory experiments in both Australia and the U.S.A. have succeeded in producing coal in a few hours under high pressure, turning wood at first into lignite, and with further pressure into coal, the necessary heat being generated by the pressure.[18]

The formation of coal in the Colorado Plateau (U.S.A.) has been dated by radiometric techniques, as reported in Science, where Robert V. Gentry wrote: "Such extraordinary values admit the possibility that . . . coalification could possibly have occurred within the past several thousand years".[19] The fact that fossils are found in coal seams indicates that seams were formed very rapidly under great pressure, allowing no time for animals and plants to decompose.

Oil has been made under laboratory conditions from biomass by heat and pressure.[20] An article entitled "Youngest Oil Deposit Found Below Gulf of California" said that radiocarbon had dated it to 4,240 years old, but "the oil may actually be even younger . . . between 500 and 3,000 years younger".[21] This report not only confirms that oil is not old, but also admits the uncertainty of radiocarbon dating methods.

Oil from the oil-rich Gulf of Mexico was reported to have been dated as being but thousands of years old.[22] Another obvious reason why oil deposits are not millions of years old is the phenomenon of oil 'gushers'. These are evidence that the oil deposits are under tremendous pressure. Whether the pressure is caused by gas formation or by the geostatic pressure of the overburden of rock, in the course of millions of years there would have been a leakage to relieve the pressure. That such leakage has not taken place to any significant degree suggests that the formation is not old. Oil deposits are sometimes located by seepage from deposits under pressure, and the fact that only a minor loss of pressure has yet taken place is evidence that the deposit is of comparatively recent formation.

**The geologic column**

Students and the general public are commonly given the impression, by means of illustrations of the 'Geologic Column', that layers of rock are to be found in a certain order, and that they constitute a sort of clock, or timetable, of the past. Each stratum is commonly given a date for its deposition. A noted geologist, John Woodmorappe, has this to say about it: "80% to 85% of the Earth's land surface does not have even three geologic periods appearing in 'correct' consecutive order ... it becomes an overall exercise of gargantuan special pleading and imagination for the evolutionary uniformitarian paradigm to maintain that there ever were geologic periods".[23]

It is a fact of geology that, somewhere in the world, rocks of every geologic 'period' lie directly on the basement rocks in which there are no fossils. It is also a fact of geology that nowhere in the world can the geologic column be found complete as presented in the textbooks.

For example, evolutionists regard trilobites as among the earliest living creatures; and, because their fossils abound in the Cambrian rocks, these rocks are put at the foot of the geologic column. But what are the facts? In British Columbia, at Field in the Rocky Mountains, in the highest part of this great mountain range, are tremendous beds of fossil trilobites and other fossils of so-called primitive creatures. Here the Cambrian rocks are clearly not the lowest rocks.

If the geologic column has been gradually building up for hundreds of millions of years, there ought to be evidence among the fossils of very many meteorites in the strata. While it is true that many meteors burn up on entering the earth's atmosphere, yet some get through each year. There should be millions of them hiding in among the fossils, but there are very few indeed. This would seem to be good evidence of a recently formed earth.

The presence of fossils in rock strata is good evidence that the strata did not take millions of years to form, but were laid down rapidly. Fossils can only be formed by abnormal conditions in which the remains of living plants or creatures have been covered in a manner that excludes air, bacteria and decay yet permits the action of water and trace elements to act upon the remains. It is obvious that the process was very rapid and the result of a cataclysmic event.

### Cosmic dust

Unseen by most of us, vast quantities of micrometeoric dust from space settle on the earth and on the moon. Whereas this dust, as it settles on the earth, is absorbed by the soil or blown into the sea, the moon does not have such conditions. Astronaut Neil Armstrong, who went to the moon, is reported to have expressed great fear of landing in a deep layer of cosmic dust. "The moon was for many years characterised as having a thick layer of dust covering its surface, into which an object would sink if it landed on the moon".[24]

What happened when the astronauts landed? They found that the dust was minimal, and no problem at all for them. But astrophysicist Dr Donald DeYoung commented: "The Moon dust problem has not gone away! The absence of lunar dust is an evidence for a more recently created Moon than claimed by evolutionists". The problem now is, Why so little cosmic dust if the moon is millions of years old?

Cosmic dust is also attracted to the sun, which absorbs it. *New Scientist* reported that "the Sun cleans dust away so effectively that it should have cleared out the Solar System long ago".[25] The obvious inference from this statement is that, since there is still cosmic dust around in space, the sun cannot have been cleaning it up for millions of years, as supposed, but that the solar system has had a limited life, perhaps only some thousands of years.

"Why did you bring the hoover, Bud?"

# THE TIME FACTOR

### The appearance of maturity

It is undeniable that the geographical features of the earth have an appearance of maturity. Could it have been created with this characteristic? Unless conditions on earth had been right for life at the beginning, life would not have survived. Those conditions include a mature soil in which plants could grow, a mature atmosphere having the right mix of gases for both plant and animal life, a mature water system, and a life-sustaining source of light and heat. Without such features Planet Earth would have been sterile. Such a combination of the essentials for life cannot be explained as a chance occurrence.

That the first plant life was mature from the beginning is made clear from the record: "herb yielding seed after his kind, and the tree yielding fruit" (Gen. 1:12). That the first creatures were mature when placed upon the earth is clear from the record: "fowl that may fly . . . and every living creature that moveth . . . Be fruitful, and multiply" (vv. 20-22). This is not a description of seeds or eggs that would develop into mature plants and creatures, but of actual maturity, with an appearance of maturity. "Male and female created He them . . . Be fruitful, and multiply" (vv. 27,28) is a description of a mature man and woman. It is certainly not a picture of embryonic, or infantile, male and female. They were mature, with the capability of reproduction.

It is not unreasonable, therefore, to see Planet Earth as being created mature, ready to receive life, with an appearance of age. To the accusation that this would have been deception on the part of the Creator, the obvious answer is that, since the creative process has been plainly described in the Genesis account, there has been no deception.

---

*"**WELL,** what about evolution? It certainly has the function of knowledge, but does it convey any? We are back to the question I have been putting to people: 'Is there any one thing you can tell me about evolution?' The absence of answers seems to suggest that it is true that evolution does not convey any knowledge"* (Palaeontologist Dr Colin Patterson speaking to the American Museum of Natural History, 5 November 1981, Transcript 3).

## References

1. *Scientific American* (Aug. 1989), p. 78.
2. *Nature* (9 July 1987), p. 111.
3. *New Scientist* (23 Sept. 1982), p. 829.
4. *Nature* (2 Nov. 1978), p. 56.
5. *Nature* (6 Jan. 1983), p. 21.
6. W. G. Stansfield (1977), *The Science of Evolution*, Macmillan, p. 80.
7. *American Journal of Science* (Jan. 1976), p. 48.
8. *Encyclopaedia Britannica* (1958), Vol. 10, p. 168.
9. Stephen J. Gould (1977), *Paleobiology*, Vol. 3(I), p. 34.
10. *New Scientist* (16 Aug. 1979), p. 516.
11. *Nature* (16 Sept. 1989), p. 32.
12. *Chemical and Engineering News* (11 Oct. 1976), p. 40.
13. Sturla Fridriksson (1975), Preface to *Surtsey*.
14. Sigurdur Thorarinsson (1964), *Surtsey*.
15. *Journal of Geophysical Research* (13 July 1968).
16. *New Scientist* (30 Sept. 1989), p. 26.
17. *Nature* (27 Feb. 1986), p. 795.
18. *Nature* (9 June 1988), p. 549.
19. *Science* (15 Oct. 1976), pp. 315-7.
20. *Science Digest* (July 1973), p. 77.
21. *New Scientist* (6 April 1991), p. 19.
22. *Science* (24 Oct. 1952).
23. *American Association of Petroleum Geologists* (Aug. 1956), p. 1805.
24. R. T. Dixon (1971), *Dynamic Astronomy*, Prentice Hall, p. 146.
25. *New Scientist* (1 May 1991), p. 3.

# 6

# THEISTIC EVOLUTION

One attempt to reconcile the Genesis account of creation with current scientific thought and theory is known as theistic evolution. This concept suggests that the Creator used a process of evolution to diversify the forms of life on earth. From a careful perusal of Charles Darwin's *Origin of Species* it would seem that he may have had some such idea, for he did not seek to eliminate the Creator as most of his followers did.

That there is a variation among living things, whether in vegetation or in creatures, is undeniable. A glance at the wide variations to be seen in human beings, or dogs, or potatoes, is evidence of this factor of variability. Yet it is also evident that such variations are members of a family which is interfertile within the family. There is no evidence that monkeys ever became humans, or that reptiles became birds, as proposed by the theory of evolution.

The theistic evolutionist, in his enthusiasm for his theory, seeks to mould the Genesis account to his scientific theory, regardless of the fact that the theory is unproved, and ignoring the implications of the theory which have led its advocates into atheism. The theistic evolution concept has been stated thus: "In the light of modern science the early chapters of Genesis can no longer be regarded as either a literal history or literal science".

**The theistic argument**
The advocate of this view will argue that the Genesis account was intended to identify the Creator, but not to reveal how creation took

place. In reply it must be pointed out that the identity of the Creator is stated in verse 1, and so by this argument the following thirty verses are superfluous. Actually, the way by which creation took place is spelled out clearly nine times in the first chapter, in the statement, "And God said ...". The Creator's power and authority was such that He only had to speak and it was done.

It has been suggested that the creation account is a poem, or allegory, rather than an historical record. It is certainly not written in the form of a typical Hebrew poem. If it is merely an allegory, why is so much detail given? Why do the many references to the wonders of creation in later scriptures all speak of it as a specific event in history?

The attitude of a famous evolutionist to the theistic concept may be to the point. T. H. Huxley wrote: "It is vain to discuss a supposed coincidence between Genesis and science, unless we have first settled, on the one hand, what Genesis says, and on the other hand, what science says".

With this observation we can heartily agree. What Genesis says has been written down for thousands of years, and has not varied one iota. What science says, or rather what scientists say, is a constantly moving picture, changing with the times, and far from a settled view. Almost every year a new theory of evolution is formulated. Its advocate invariably begins by pointing out the errors and shortcomings of previous theories. It is impossible therefore to settle what science says.

The well-known evolutionist writer G. G. Simpson wrote this comment on theistic evolution: "The attempt to build an evolutionary theory mingling mysticism and science has only tended to vitiate the science. I strongly suspect that it has been equally damaging on the religious side, but here I am less qualified to judge".[1]

A very perceptive observer of the scene wrote: "... no biblically derived religion can really be reconciled with the fundamental assertion of Darwinian theory. Chance and design are antithetical concepts, and the decline in religious belief can probably be attributed more to the propagation and advocacy by the intellectual and scientific community of the Darwinian version of evolution than to any other single factor".[2]

# THEISTIC EVOLUTION

*"IN all this great museum there is not a particle of evidence of the transmutation of species"* (Dr Etheridge of the British Museum of Natural History).

●

*"LIFE represents matter organised into systems of great complexity. How such orderly aggregates could develop in the first place, persist and continue to become more complex, is not so easily explainable in terms of the generally accepted laws of the physical sciences"* (Fred Kohler in *Evolution and Human Destiny*, p. 14). The organisation, complexity and laws evident in nature speak of an intelligence rather than of randomness.

●

**A REVIEW** of a book in *New Scientist* speaks of *"the dogmatic self-righteousness of scientists"*. What was needed, the author says, *"was a little more willingness to listen rather than to lay down the law, a little more humility. Scientists stand in need of these Christian virtues just as much as preachers do"* (*New Scientist*, 26 August 1989, p. 61).

●

*"AS FAR as the Universe is concerned we will never be able to deduce the nature of the whole from the parts . . . The Universe, on the most fundamental level, is an undissectible whole"* (*New Scientist*, 6 April 1991, p. 46). Here is a frank admission of why science cannot see the truth of Divine creation of the universe: because it is so busy scrutinising this little part or that little part that it cannot see the wood for the trees.

## Three alternatives

The theistic evolutionist proposes three alternatives as possible ways in which the Creator might have made use of a process of evolution:
1. that the Creator produced a primeval living cell which then evolved into the vast variety of living forms as seen today;
2. that variations in living forms were thrown up by chance, which the Creator used for His purpose;
3. that the Creator manipulated the process of variation so that His purpose was finally achieved.

None of these three propositions is acceptable to the believer in the accuracy of the Divine record of Scripture. None of these three propositions is acceptable to the evolutionist, who sees life as an accident of nature without any need for a Creator. The theistic evolutionist fails to satisfy the requirements of both the Genesis record and the theory of evolution. He is in the unhappy position of casting doubt on a very specific Divine record, which was confirmed and endorsed by no less an authority than Jesus Christ. He fails to please the evolutionist by introducing an element of miracle into a severely materialistic theory.

The serious implications of this theory have been stated thus: "The reinterpretation of relevant Bible passages is the key to the whole problem".[3] Thus science has to be regarded as the standard by which the Bible is to be judged and reconciled, notwithstanding the continually changing theories of science, which fail to provide a definitive model.

## Can evolution be seen in Genesis?
1. No hidden clue to a process of evolution can be seen in the power of the Creator to create at His command: "And God said . . .".
2. No millions of years can be seen in the six-times repeated period of an evening-morning day (Heb. *yom*). If a longer time had been involved the Hebrew word *olam* would have been appropriate.
3. The statement in Genesis, repeated ten times, that each kind of life was created to reproduce "after his kind", is scientifically accurate and is a denial of any evolutionary process.

# THEISTIC EVOLUTION    123

4. It is stated that creation was completed (Gen. 2:1) and is not a continuing process. Evolution is supposed to be a continuing process, although it is not observable scientifically.
5. The theory of evolution is based on an eternal struggle to survive, whereas the Bible advocates submission in humility to a loving and caring Creator Who has created life for an eternal purpose.
6. Man is not a jumped-up animal, but was a new creation, formed out of the earth, and destined to return to the earth unless he accepts the Creator's plan of redemption through the sacrifice of Jesus. No animal has been offered such a hope.
7. That man is not an evolved animal was stated clearly by Jesus when he said: "from the beginning of the creation God made them male and female" (Mk. 10:6).

To summarise, there is no inkling of a process of evolution in the Creator's own account of His creation. To try to reconcile the Genesis account with the materialistic philosophy of evolution leads to ignoring the Creator's inspired record of the beginning of life, and missing the purpose of life, which is the main theme of the Bible. While Genesis is not a scientific treatise, yet it cannot be faulted by science. The established laws of biology confirm the profound statements of this simply stated Divine record in Genesis. There is no need to attempt to reconcile it with scientific theory, for theories come, and theories go.

## Genesis and Jesus Christ

The first two chapters of Genesis, with the account of creation and the origin of man, are entirely consistent with the rest of the Holy Scriptures, and are indeed the basis of God's plan for man as elucidated during the succeeding centuries and brought to a climax in the sacrifice of Jesus, man's redeemer. The accuracy of the Genesis record is vital to an understanding of the Christian faith.

Jesus regarded Genesis as historical and Divinely inspired, as shown by his bitter comment on the attitude of the Jews to the written Word of God: "If they hear not Moses and the prophets, neither will they be persuaded, though one rose from the dead" (Lk. 16:31). Jesus had no qualms about quoting from the Genesis record: "Have ye not read, that He Which made them at the beginning made them male and female . . . ?" (Mt. 19:4). Jesus was not quoting a myth, but a historical fact to prove his point.

The Apostle Paul, addressing a pagan audience at Athens, spoke of "God that made the world and all things therein" (Acts 17:24). Later he wrote: "The first man Adam was made a living soul" (1 Cor. 15:45); and to Timothy he wrote: "For Adam was first formed, then Eve" (1 Tim. 2:13). The early Christian writers of the first century A.D. made frequent references to the creation account as being historical, truthful and believable. There is no trace of a theory of evolution in any of the Bible references to creation.

Unless the first chapters of Genesis are taken as historical, there is no reasonable, satisfactory or scientific explanation of the origin of life on earth. Likewise, there is no other logical explanation of the origin of sin, and its consequence, death. The repeated statements that the Creator saw that what He had created was "very good" are the reverse of the evolutionary concept of an upward struggle from crudity to complexity. A look at the history of nature would show the reverse of this to be true, in accordance with the Law of Entropy.

"Wherefore, as by one man sin entered into the world, and death by sin; and so death passed upon all men, for that all have sinned . . ." (Rom. 5:12). This is the simple, yet awful, factual state of mankind, which can only be explained and understood by an acceptance of the Genesis account of how sin entered into the world, by the disobedience of the first man.

The logical result of trying to adapt Genesis to the theory of evolution was pointed out very clearly in these words: "Evolution destroys utterly and finally the very reason Jesus's earthly life was supposedly made necessary. Destroy Adam and Eve and original sin, and in the rubble you will find the sorry remains of the Son of God . . . If Jesus was not the redeemer who died for our sins, and this is what evolution means, then Christianity is nothing".[4]

### The rise of theistic evolution

The Apostle Paul could see a conflict between the Divinely inspired record of creation and the pagan concept which elevated the creature to a higher place than the Creator. Hence he wrote of those

# THEISTIC EVOLUTION

who "changed the truth of God into a lie, and worshipped and served the creature more than the Creator" (Rom. 1:25). To place human reasoning on a higher plane than Divine revelation is to deny God and His revealed Word. This is the basic error of theistic evolution.

The attitude of many religious organisations is ambiguous. While making a profession of accepting the Bible, they try to adapt it to the latest scientific theory. For example, this century, the pronouncements of the Catholic Church have vacillated. The Catholic Encyclical *Humani Generis* of Pope Paul XII maintained that Adam was created by God from the earth. "Whenever such conjectural opinions are directly or indirectly opposed to doctrine revealed by God, then a claim of this kind [evolution] can in no circumstances be admitted". Then *Sacrae Theologiae Summa* stated: "The evolution of man's body is far from being an established fact, it is in fact a mere hypothesis, on the probability of which even the scientists hold different opinions".[5]

By way of contrast, the Catholic Truth Society says: "The Church says there is nothing in this notion [evolution] intrinsically repugnant either to the scripture or to faith"; and, "if anyone chooses to make it a purely personal belief, he may".[6] Hence popular Catholic publications such as the *Reader's Digest* and the *National Geographic* magazine, while betraying a Catholic bias, also promulgate the theory of evolution without question, as if it is gospel truth.

The situation was put neatly by the Apostle Paul, when he wrote: "your faith should not stand in the wisdom of men, but in the power of God" (1 Cor. 2:5). He further warned: "Beware lest any man spoil you through philosophy and vain deceit, after the tradition of men, after the rudiments of the world, and not after Christ" (Col. 2:8). To his beloved Timothy he wrote: ". . . avoiding profane and vain babblings, and oppositions of science falsely so called: which some professing have erred concerning the faith" (1 Tim. 6:20,21).

The historical fact that the theory of evolution has led many to a denial of the Creator and to utter atheism should be a warning to believers not to toy with this theory. Theistic evolution is a compromise that satisfies neither faith in God nor human philosophy.

## References

1. G. G. Simpson (1964), *This View of Life*, Harcourt Brace, New York, p. 232.
2. Dr M. Denton (1985), *Evolution—A Theory in Crisis*, Burnett Books, 1985, p. 66.
3. M. R. Johnson (1988), *Genesis, Geology and Catastrophism*, Paternoster Press, p. 11.
4. *The American Atheist* (Feb. 1978), p. 30.
5. *Sacrae Theologiae Summa*, Vol. 2 (1952), p. 507.
6. Catholic Truth Society pamphlet R144, p. 18.

# 20 SCIENTIFIC FACTS SELDOM TAUGHT TO STUDENTS

**1** The origin of life is unknown to science. The Law of Biogenesis observes that life only comes from life. Louis Pasteur proved scientifically that life does not come from non-life, a fact that is the basis of the food-canning industry to this day.

**2** Natural selection, the supposed basis of evolution, can only select from existing characteristics and does not produce new genetic material.

**3** Mutations, said to be the source of new genetic material, are harmful to life and often lethal. Deliberately induced mutations in over 3,000 consecutive generations of fruit flies have failed to produce a better fruit fly, or to increase its viability.

**4** As Charles Darwin admitted, there is no actual evidence of any species having developed into another species.

**5** Acquired characteristics cannot be inherited. For example, a one-armed man will not have one-armed children, as Lamarck's theory falsely assumed in order to account for evolution.

**6** The variations within each species are all explicable by Mendel's laws of genetics, and variations are limited, as any breeder of plants or animals knows.

**7** All known species (several million) appear fully developed with all vital organs fully operational. There are no part-formed eyes, half-developed intestines or evolving feathers.

**8** Each human brain contains about one hundred thousand billion electrical connections (more than can be found in all the world's electrical appliances), a complexity that could not possibly have been produced by chance.

**9** Many animals possess sophisticated equipment that science has been unable to replicate: the radar system of bats, the sonar of whales and dolphins, the electro-detection system of the platypus, the aerodynamics of hummingbirds, the navigation systems of many birds, and the amazing self-repair system of most forms of life. Such sophisticated facilities required a superintelligence to install.

**10** While single-celled creatures are numerous, there are none with two, three, four or even twenty cells. Thus there is no evolutionary sequence from single-celled to multi-celled creatures.

**11** The genetic code in every form of life is a precise set of information for the development and activity of that form of life, accompanied by elaborate transmission and duplication systems, without which life would cease. This complexity cannot be accounted for by chance, but testifies to intelligent design in every form of life.

**12** The genetic information encoded in each cell in the DNA, if written out in detail, would require as many as 4,000 large volumes of closely printed text. This is no accident of nature.

**13** The DNA helix in each cell requires twenty different proteins for its structure. These specific proteins can only be produced under the direction of the information in the DNA; therefore the whole complex system must have been formed complete from the beginning of life.

**14** Amino acids formed synthetically are either right-handed or left-handed. The amino acids in all forms of life are all left-handed, without exception, clear evidence of intelligent selection and design.

**15** Symbiosis, the interdependence of two forms of life, such as the fig tree and the fig-gall wasp, the yucca plant and Pronuba moth, pollen plants and the bee, each dependent for life upon the other, must have been formed complete at the same time.

**16** Fossils are evidence of extinctions, not of new forms of life. Their condition is evidence of very rapid burial, while many polystrate fossils indicate that several strata were laid rapidly round the upright fossil.

**17** At the base of the fossil record there is evidence of many highly complex creatures, but no evidence of an evolutionary sequence.

**18** The so-called 'missing link' between one form of life and another requires many millions of missing links if a slow evolutionary process did actually take place. All are missing.

**19** Most dinosaurs are known only by their tracks impressed on mud that turned to stone. In Russia, horse-hoof tracks and human footprints have been found alongside dinosaur tracks, contrary to the evolutionary scenario.

**20** Language studies have revealed that ancient languages were far more complex than modern languages in their form, syntax, cases, genders and tenses. Of the thirty-six known cases of feral children, reared without human contact, it is evident that language is not inherent but is learned from other humans. Language did not evolve but was an endowment from creation.

*"Have ye not known? have ye not heard?
Hath it not been told you from the
   beginning?
Have ye not understood from the foundations
   of the earth?
It is He that sitteth upon the circle of the
   earth,
   and the inhabitants thereof are as
      grasshoppers;
That stretcheth out the heavens as a curtain,
   and spreadeth them out as a tent to dwell
      in . . .
To whom then will ye liken Me, or shall I be
   equal?
   saith the Holy One.
Lift up your eyes on high, and behold Who
   hath created these things,
   that bringeth out their host by number:
He calleth them all by names
By the greatness of His might, for that He is
   strong in power; not one faileth . . .
Hast thou not known? hast thou not heard,
That the everlasting God, the* LORD, *the
   Creator of the ends of the earth,
   fainteth not, neither is weary?
There is no searching of His understanding."*

(Isaiah 40:21,22,25,26,28)

# SUBJECT INDEX

# SCRIPTURE INDEX

Compiled by Gill Nicholls

# SUBJECT INDEX

## A

Adam   20, 124, 125
Aerobic life   42
Agassiz, Louis   81
Amino acids   30, 31, 32, 50, 52, 101, 103
Angels   21
Ants   7, 64–5
Army ants   65
Asimov, Isaac   55
Atomic structure   45, 100
Atoms   32, 33, 45
ATP   50

## B

Babylonian creation myth   18
Bacteria   14
'Bar code of life'   51–4
Bees   7, 61–4. *See also* Honey bee
Big Bang theory   20, 36, 43
Biogenesis, Law of   12, 26, 29, 33, 68
'Blueprint for life'   60
Brain   55–7, 104, 105

## C

Caterpillars   63
Cell   8, 48–54, 52, 102. *See also* Living cells
  division   25, 101
  structure   49
Chaos   36, 37
Christ   7. *See also* Jesus Christ
Coelacanth   109–10
'Cold dark matter' theory   43
Conservation of Energy, Law of   99
Cosmic dust   32, 116

# INDEX

Cosmology   113
Creation   11, 12, 13, 17–22, 26, 37, 68–75, 108, 119–20, 124.
   *See also* Divine creation
Creator   11, 12, 13, 21, 29, 33, 37, 39, 43, 57, 58, 60, 64, 65, 67, 68–75, 94, 100, 117, 119–25

## D

Darlington, C. D.   79
Darwin, Charles   24, 30, 58, 80, 80–1, 83, 86, 87, 90, 106, 107, 119
Darwinian theory of evolution   7, 24, 79, 86, 120
Deoxyribonucleic acid   48
Desert ants   65
Diatomite   111
Divine creation   13, 20, 23, 33, 63, 121. *See also* Creation
DNA   31, 48, 49–53, 101–2

## E

Ears   59
Einstein, Albert   35, 46
Electrochemical impulses   55
Electromagnetic theory of light   13
Electrons   45
Elements   45
Entropy, Law of   99, 124
*Enuma Elish*   18
Enzymes   50, 102
Eve   20, 71, 124
Evolution, theory of   11, 12, 52, 79, 98. *See also* Darwinian theory of evolution
Eyes   57–8

## F

Firmament   18, 41
First Cause   37, 100, 103
Fossils   63, 67, 86–91, 109, 110–11, 114, 115
Frazer, James G.   17
Fruit flies   93

## G

Gamma rays  92
Genes  25, 52, 92, 93, 94, 102
Genetic code  50, 54, 60, 64, 65
Genetic coding system  50
Genetic material  49
Genome  101
Geologic column  114–5
Geology  87, 115
Glia cells  56
Glucose  50
Gravity, Law of  37

## H

Harmony of orbits of planets  41, 46
Honey bee  61–4, 103
'Hopeful monster' theory  90
Hoyle, Fred  50, 103
Human genetic code  50, 102
*Humani Generis*  125
Huxley, Aldous  84
Huxley, Andrew  29, 99
Huxley, T. H.  14, 24, 120
Hybridism  106–7
Hydrogen  45

## I

Index Fossil System  109–10
Inheritance, Law of  106

## J

Jeans, James  35, 100
Jesus Christ  21, 24, 73–4, 122, 123–4. *See also* Christ

## K

Kepler, Johannes  37, 46
Kitchen, Kenneth  18
Koestler, Arthur  93

## INDEX

## L

Last Adam  75
Living cells  26, 30, 48, 52, 101.  *See also* cell

## M

Macroevolution  90, 93, 95
Mendel's law of inheritance  106
Meteorites  32, 115
Microevolution  93
Microscopic life  25
"Might is right" principle  24
Miller, Stanley  30, 31
Missing link  87-9
Mitochondria  48
Mitochondrial DNA  106
Molecular signature  25
Monera  30
Moon  18, 44, 69, 70, 116
Moon dust  116
Moore, Patrick  46
Motor neuron  56
Muggeridge, Malcolm  84
Muller, H. J.  93
Mutagens  92
Mutations  90, 92-5
Myoglobin  30
Myth  17-22
Mythoplasm  17, 18, 19

## N

Natural selection  58, 79, 81, 94, 95, 105
Natural symmetry  46-7
Nematode  104
Neo-Darwinism  95
Neon  45
Neurons  56
Neutrons  92
New Creation  73-4

Newton, Isaac  *37, 46, 58, 80*
Nitrogen  *42*
Nucleic acids  *49, 102*
Nucleotides  *50, 53, 101, 102–3*
Nucleus  *45, 48, 100*

## O

Ocean tides  *45*
Origin of life  *12, 29–34, 50, 80, 98, 102, 103, 124*
*Origin of Species*  *7, 81, 82, 87, 90, 119*
Oxygen  *39, 42–4, 56, 69*

## P

Palaeontology  *87*
Pasteur, Louis  *12, 14, 29, 103*
Paul the Apostle  *72, 74, 124, 125*
Peppered Moth  *95, 96*
Planet Earth  *8, 11, 39, 42–7, 68, 69, 70, 71, 74, 117*
Planets  *36, 37, 43, 44, 46*
Pollution  *27, 73, 96*
Polypeptides  *32*
Polystrate fossils  *111*
Popper, Karl  *79*
Primeval soup  *30, 103*
*Principia*  *37*
Proteins  *25, 32, 50, 52, 101–3*
Protons  *45*
'Punctuated Equilibrium' theory  *90, 94*

## R

Radio-dating  *108*
Radiocarbon dating  *112, 114*
Radiometric dating  *109, 112, 114*
Random mutations  *63, 93*
Rational design  *46*
Relativity, theory of  *35*
Retina  *57, 58*
RNA  *49–50*

## S

Seeds  *100, 106*
Serpent  *71*
Simpson, G. G.  *88, 89, 120*
Smith, William  *109*
Solar system  *13, 37–9, 41, 43, 44, 46, 68, 116*
Spence, Lewis  *17*
Spiders  *63, 65–7, 110*
Spontaneous generation  *12, 14, 29, 30, 72, 102, 103*
Sumerian creation myth  *18*
Survival of the fittest  *24, 27, 95, 97, 105*
Symmetry of design  *47*
Synthetic molecules  *31*

## T

*The Golden Bough*  *17*
Theistic evolution  *12, 119–25*
Theory of evolution  *120, 123*
Thermodynamics
   First Law of  *99*
   Second Law of  *35, 99, 105*
Tides  *45*
Transmutation of species  *121*
Tree of life  *74*
Trilobites  *115*

## U

Uranium  *45*

## W

Water  *26, 39, 44, 69, 117*

## X

X-rays  *92, 93*

# SCRIPTURE INDEX

**Genesis**
1     21
1:2    29
1:12   26,117
1:20-22  117
1:21   26
1:25   26
1:27,28  117
2:1    123
2:7    19

**Numbers**
14:21   26,72,76

**Job**
26:7    41
38:7    21

**Psalms**
19:1    41
33:6    21
37:9,29   76
94:8,9   58
97:7    21
103:20   21
115:16   76
139:14   53,102

**Proverbs**
8:27    46
8:30    46
11:31   76
20:12   58

**Isaiah**
40:12,13   37
40:21,22,25,26,28  130
45:12   39
45:18   72,74,76
65:17   19
66:2    26
66:22   73

**Matthew**
5:5    26,76
6:10    74
19:4    124

**Mark**
10:6    123

**Luke**
1:17    26
16:31   123

**John**
3:16,17   74
17:3    74

**Acts**
17:24   124
17:25   33,72

**Romans**
1:20    72
1:25    125
5:12    124
6:23    74,76
9:26    73

**1 Corinthians**
2:5    125
15:45   124

**2 Corinthians**
5:17    73

**Ephesians**
2:10    73
4:24    73

**Colossians**
2:8    125

138

**1 Timothy**
2:13    *124*
6:20,21    *125*

**Hebrews**
1:6    *21*

**1 Peter**
1:13    *76*

**2 Peter**
3:9    *73*
3:13    *73*

**Revelation**
2:7    *74*
4:11    *73*